Pitching to Win

Targeting Your Presentation at the Heart of the Prospect

Jeff Woodard

ISBN: 978-0-9827346-0-5

Jeff Woodard

52 Woodgrove Ave

Singapore 738247

Jeff@jnwoodard.com

www.jeff-woodard.com, www.woodard.asia, www.jwoodard.net, www.woodard.co, www.thewinningpitch.info, and www.thewinningpitch.biz

Social Media: www.Facebook.com/Jeff.Woodard

www.Twitter.com/CoachJeffW

Connect with me on "LinkedIn"

Limits of Liability and Disclaimer of Warranty

Warning – Disclaimer

After all the effort, discussions, meetings, and late nights, how many sales presentations do you or your team actually win? Do you suffer from these common pitching problems?

- Lack of process to qualify 'what to bid for' and 'what not to bid for'

- Presentations with too much detail

- Not seen as a real team

- Lack of differentiation; no clear benefits understood by the audience

- No clear flow, poor sequencing of ideas, not persuasive

- Poor time management, audience loses focus and gets bored

Whether you are making persuasive presentations to million-dollar accounts or inside your own company, this book explores these common problems and more, and offers succinct, practical, and proven advice to solve them.

Testimonials for Jeff Woodard

Jeff's ability to teach, inspire, and build confidence is known throughout our industry in Asia. I have personally worked with Jeff in building more powerful board and investor presentations, and used him to build a higher performing sales organization. He carries a wealth of experience and a wide range of proven techniques that are delivered in a concise distinctive manner and will provide you with both personal and professional growth.

Tom McCabe,
Managing Director, DBS Bank Singapore, and
member of the Chicago Graduate School of Business Asia Advisory Board.

Connecting with people is an essential part of life not just from the perspective of business but in all everyday situations. The thoughts and processes put forward by Jeff Woodard are both incisive and decisive.

Gerald Miranda,
CEO Zenith Media Malaysia

All our staff have attended Jeff's multi-day training sessions on presentation skills, and we work with him to tailor conference speeches. He is a fantastic coach who helped us to communicate to our clients and potential clients much more effectively. Our seniors are also coached by Jeff to improve their overall business and selling effectiveness, internally and externally – with excellent results!

Piers Tonge,
Vice President, Schlumberger Consulting Services, Asia-Pacific

"The quality of our communications directly affects the quality of our lives." How about you? Are you maximizing your persuasive communication opportunities?

To get clear on your personal and team goals and what it will take to get the winning edge, contact me about setting up a free 30-minute session where you will walk away with specific steps about what you can do to achieve your goals.

Contact Jeff at **jeff@jnwoodard.com** or call +65 9786-3062

www.jwoodard.net
www.jeff-woodard.com
www.woodard.asia
www.thewinningpitch.info
www.thewinningpitch.biz

For Lori,
the love of my life.
I married up.

Help a child to learn –

10% of all royalties are donated to the International Rescue Committee. Please visit http://www.theirc.org.

No book is the product of one person. I have had many teachers and mentors throughout the years - in the flesh, in books and audios, and virtually online. To my family, friends, colleagues, and clients who supported, challenged, and cajoled me along the way, I offer humble gratitude. I would not have done it without you. A few special thank you's to:

-   my Mother for her unyielding attitude, unassuming love and support, my brothers and special spouses who continue to teach me, my children Zac, Megan, and Ian.

-   Jan-Erik who wholeheartedly supported The Winning Pitch and therefore inspired me to move ahead during some dark hours.

-   Bryan, Tom, Lee, Libby, Vivek, Gerald, Dale, Steve, Henrik, Maureen, and the others who have challenged, supported, and who continue to help me grow.

-   David & Lana, Rodney, Joey, Paul, Trey, Scott, and others who have nurtured me in very important ways.

About the Author

Jeff Woodard is a leading expert on effective presentation skills, leadership image development, and communications and media skills. He is a founder and partner in Simitri Pte Ltd, in Singapore, a communications consultancy with offices across Asia. Simitri develops and delivers unique products and services to enable clients to accelerate success, both personally and professionally. Clients include executives at many of the top companies in the world, including Dell Computer, Microsoft, Standard Chartered Bank, JP Morgan, Deutsche Bank, Schlumberger, and BHP Billiton. He has mentored and coached business leaders in dozens of countries. Jeff's knowledge and expertise make him a sought-after corporate communications speaker and coach.

Jeff coaches executives to clarify their messages, and to present them with impact for IPO road shows, stock analyst and investor presentations, board meetings, large annual business meetings and trade shows, as well as for internal and external events. His techniques have helped thousands of people better develop and deliver their mission-critical business presentations.

An expert on formulating message content and teaching clear and passionate delivery, Jeff's focus includes executive training and coaching to quickly improve his clients' awareness, understanding, and impact in all areas of their lives. Jeff co-developed The Winning Pitch Workshop, which consists of two days of training followed by one to one pitch coaching. He and his partners have delivered it successfully to hundreds of business people over the past four years, in the US, Europe, Asia, and the Middle East.

With a strong international business background, Jeff focuses on bottom-line results. He holds a degree in Electrical Engineering, and an MBA. He is a charter member of the Asia Professional Speaker's Association of Singapore, and a member of the International Coach Federation.

Jeff believes in giving more value than expected, and is dedicated to his motto, "The quality of our communications directly affects the quality of our lives." We are communicating most of our waking hours; we can always learn to do it better.

A father of two sons and one daughter, Jeff has lived and worked internationally for 20 years; he currently lives with his family in Singapore.

Contents

Contents

Preface

*"Make thyself a craftsman in speech,
for thereby thou shalt gain the upper hand."*
- Ancient Egyptian Tomb inscription

*"The fact is, everyone is in sales. Whatever area you work in,
you do have clients and you do need to sell."*
- Jay Abraham

This is a book on developing and delivering an effective pitch. But what is a pitch? The dictionary defines *pitch* as "promotion by means of an argument and demonstration." So a pitch is a sales presentation — a presentation wherein you attempt to persuade another person to do something — to take an action. We are pitching something every day — any time we are attempting to create change.

You are pitching when you are meeting a new client. You are pitching whether you are asking the boss for more headcount or delivering a multimillion-dollar RFP response to a multinational account.

Whether you are speaking to an audience of one or hundreds; whether you call them sales presentations or beauty pageants; or whether it's a monthly business presentation, proposal response, or an analyst talk, there is much in this book for you.

This book will show you how to dramatically improve your results by making your pitches more relevant, impactful, and memorable.

These techniques come from practical business experience. They have been proven successful in the meeting room, the boardroom, and the classroom. They are results-oriented.

Very few people speak and present well. Good communicators are universally admired. If you work to put yourself in that select group, your success will be much more likely. John Howard once said that a leader is an encourager and a persuader and an advocate. This book will help you encourage and persuade and advocate better for your company — and for yourself.

> **Learn from those who have done it. Find out how they did it. Model that success.**
>
> **In 1789, a young Mozart heard a performance of one of Bach's motets — a highly varied choral musical composition in several parts. When Mozart heard the piece, he was spellbound, and called out, "Now there is something one can learn from!"**
>
> **He then studied the multi-part manuscript carefully until he could understand exactly how the parts interacted. If a genius like Mozart can learn from others, we can too.**

How I Got Here

Why should you study and apply the techniques in this book? Why did I write it?

Those are very good questions.

The short answer is because these techniques work. They are tried and true, and have been tested successfully for years in a number of situations. They can work for you.

The longer answer comes from my experience and me. I come to the business of training and coaching from a multinational career spanning a number of countries. During this time, I have worked on, delivered, and assisted with many pitches and other presentations. I'm a businessperson, not an academic.

I have seen the development of presentations from the creation of vellums on plastic to printing on overheads to the current infatuation with PowerPoint. I have seen many, many poor presentations and some good ones. I have witnessed firsthand the lost opportunities arising from poor communications. I also have had the exhilaration of winning the big deal with a skillful and clear pitch, and I have seen audiences motivated to tears and cheers by a well-delivered motivational message. So I know the power of the presentation.

However, very few people have been trained in proper presentation techniques. I believe this is a huge need in many businesses today.

My broad business experience has created a passion within to help business people of all types create and deliver better communications. I am *firmly* convinced that the quality of our lives depends upon the quality of our communications — both professionally and personally. If I can help you to do this in some small way, then I will be rewarded many times over… and so will you!

Jeff Woodard

June 2010

Introduction

"As soon as you move one step up from the bottom, your effectiveness depends on your ability to reach others through the spoken and written word."

- Peter Drucker

Business is an activity with four specific requirements:

1. You find other businesses (i.e., people) willing to pay you to provide your service or product to them.

2. Once you have found them, you win them with your value proposition.

3. Then you keep them from going elsewhere, to another provider.

4. Finally, you grow the original value proposition in direct proportion to their growing needs.

Pitching is step 2, or the winning process. You may call it an RFP response, a sales presentation, or even a beauty contest. By whatever name, every business — large or small — will one day be required to send in a person or a team to pitch for business.

But why should a potential client pick you and your company instead of someone else? Let's face it, most people and their businesses are selling something very similar, if not identical, to a service or product available from the next supplier. But we need to sell ours.

Yes, of course we all have unique selling points, better software, more value, a more enticing overall proposition, and so on — but in truth, no one has to buy from us. Why do people buy?

When you really start to look at it, people are not entirely rational about their decisions to buy. They are influenced by their past, their emotions, their peers, and the current corporate environment. If you look at your own behavior (or your partner's or your friends' for that matter) when shopping, you'll see quite clearly that people sometimes buy frivolously — for no obviously logical reason at all. One of the truisms of sales is that "people buy with emotion, and justify with logic."

Well, the same is true when one *company* is buying the services of another. People buy from people.

But what do we do when pitching? The first tendency is to dust off our well-prepared pitch presentations and use those. We talk about our star customers, our big deals, our great team, our worldwide locations, and our fantastic products. We make rational, logical arguments. We don't tell stories. We don't talk about the prospect's needs. We don't connect.

Just like everyone else!

So what can you do to differentiate yourself and your offer from all the others — to get the *winning edge*?

I suggest you go right back to basics: "People buy from people." Customers don't care about our need to sell; they are only worried about solving their business problems! Focusing on each customer's *need to buy* is critical to understanding how we can help solve that customer's business problems.

This means putting time and effort into understanding your prospect's motivations to buy, creating empathy, asking good questions to learn about them, listening, and creating the sense that you actually have time to spend — to help them solve their problems — rather than just to sell a product.

Of course, you need to satisfy the logical needs: price, service, delivery, etc. But to win, go further.

Put on the client's hat. Walk a mile in her shoes. It's hard work at times, and it means investing time and effort to understand what the client really wants and needs. But once you have found that, your chances of winning increase dramatically.

Don't waste time rambling about how big and global you are, unless these will directly influence the customer to do business with you. Don't discuss features the prospect doesn't want or need. Now that you know her needs, go to work to craft a pitch that's pointed, focused, and hits those needs. Then polish it, practice it, and deliver it in a professional manner.

A well-organized and effective presentation that speaks to your client's needs, conveys to her the idea that, if your proposal is accepted, you will execute it in a similar, well-organized, effective, and client-focused way.

"Getting to the table" is about meeting the prospect's expressed requirements. Winning the business is about understanding the human side of your prospect, and selling to that side convincingly.

This book will give you processes, tools, and techniques to understand your prospect's need to buy — so you can meet your need to sell.

The Winning Pitch Process

*"If you train yourself in the practice of deliberately picturing your desire
and carefully examining your picture,
you will soon find that your thoughts and desires proceed in a more
orderly procession than ever before."*

- Genevieve Behrend

The Winning Pitch Process is a method your team can use immediately as a guide map to winning the business. Although pitching is presented here step by step, it is often more iterative than linear. You may believe you have finished a step, but then have to revisit it after learning more about the prospect, the opportunity, and/or the competition. A pitch is a dynamic, team-based process with many players, variables, and unknowns. For some deals, you may skip or minimize a given step. You will put much more focus on some steps than others. However, I recommend you at least visit all of the steps to ensure your team has properly qualified the deal and has done its homework before committing to the significant effort required to win.

The Winning Pitch Process

1. The Prologue

   a. To Pitch or Not to Pitch

   b. Our Team

   c. The Prospect's Team

    d.   The Competition

2.   Create the Story

    a.   Set Objectives

    b.   Develop the Message

    c.   Rehearse

3.   Deliver the Story

    a.   The Pitch

    b.   Follow Through

The Prologue

"Genius is 1 percent inspiration and 99 percent perspiration.
Accordingly a genius is often merely a talented person
who has done all of his or her homework."

- Thomas Edison

Doing Your Homework (and Office Work)

Homework is not glamorous. How often did we duck it as students? Digging out the detail is hard, time-consuming work. It's the offensive line in American football. It's the goalie in soccer. It's the golfer who hits buckets of balls in obscurity. It's the chassis of the car. It's the foundation of the house.

And, without the foundation, the house won't stand.

To Pitch or Not to Pitch

> *"Learn to say NO to the good, so you can say YES to the great."*
>
> *- Jim Rohn*

The resources required to develop proposals and pitches effectively can be significant. These resources must be applied carefully and selectively; the people will need to focus on the pitch and often will be unavailable for their usual "day job." Spreading yourself too thin is a recipe for failure; it is much better to pitch well for fewer opportunities. But saying *no* takes a great deal of bravery and confidence. In *The Effective Executive*, Peter Drucker points out that being effective means not just knowing *what* to do, it also means knowing what *not* to do. If you are confused about the type of business your company should pursue, discuss it with your boss and with the team. Be clear in what you want and don't want.

Ah, you say, but this work is *strategic*. We'll work hard, price it low, and show what we can do. It'll be the beginning of a beautiful relationship. Maybe. Be very careful about pitching for business because it's strategic. Many bad deals have been struck when a company thought the business was strategic to a long-term engagement, only to find out that the promise was a chimera. Here are some questions to ask of your team:

- Do we have the facts we need?

- How can we profile the opportunity? (see Situation Analysis below)

- How do you win more?

- How do you say no?

Endeavour to understand your best targets. A good way to do this is to profile your six current best clients. *Best* can mean volume, profit, relationship depth, product mix, or any other combination you choose. Next, identify three common attributes of these best clients. It could be size, revenue, industry position, geography, or other variables. The more of these attributes you can determine, the better you can understand your clients. Carefully note the attributes you feel make these best or key clients.

Now, refer to your prospects and map these characteristics. Are they in a certain industry; are they multinational, or do they sell in one specific area? While you may branch out, experience shows that the common denominators will usually be consistent. The principle is that, at least on paper, your best prospects resemble your best clients. A situation analysis will help you determine opportunity areas where you can add value to the prospect's business.

Situation Analysis

- Is the prospect a follower or a leader in their industry?

- Are they product-led, service-led, or a low-cost provider?

- What are their goals for the business?

- Where is their business heading?

- What are the three most important trends affecting the prospect's industry?

- What outside forces are applying pressure to their industry?

- Who are the prospect's customers, and what do they want from this company?

- Who are the prospect's competitors?

- What are the prospect's competitive strengths and weaknesses?

Now, assuming you have found some opportunity areas, follow up with these questions:

- Can we really meet the needs of the prospect?

  - In what opportunity areas do their needs "fit" with our products and services?

  - Can we perform in this area and in this environment?

  - Can we deliver on time?

  - There is no value in a great solution which misses the time frame the client needs. Underpromise and overdeliver, not the other way around.

- What is the return on investment?

  - Can we make money? What is our up-front cost?

  - How long will it take for this company to become a key client?

- What is our relationship with the client?

  - Do we have, or can we quickly establish, a relationship of value with the decision-makers? Or are we kidding ourselves, when our competitor has been strongly entrenched for years (and has married the boss's daughter, perhaps)?

When I was a young engineer, we were contacted by a prospect who offered us a huge amount of work – about 50 jobs – when we normally did one job at a time. We were impressed and enthused. What an opportunity! Not only could we ensure a good stream of revenue, we could become experts in the client's area, and help both them and us as we learned more about the area. Great! This was going to be a Strategic Client.

There was a catch. The company drove a very hard bargain. In order to win this work, we would be expected to honor discounts much greater than any other client was currently receiving – even our best clients. After hot debate, we agreed to go ahead with a "pilot" with the prospect, at very low rates. The startup and learning costs to get ready for the business were to be amortized over a lot of work, so we didn't mind this up-front investment. This first job led to another job, again at the same discount. We were moving forward! Then, the client stopped. He offered no more work. We had lowered our prices to an unprecedented level, only to find the Strategic Client didn't really exist.

Lesson:

Be very careful about doing 'strategic' work. You may find you have been simply discounting with little or no upside potential.

Summary:

- Your best prospects resemble in many ways your current best clients

- A simple situation analysis will help you understand your opportunity areas

- Beware of assuming you have found a Strategic Client – qualify carefully

Our Team

"Synergy is the highest activity of life; it creates new untapped alternatives; it values and exploits the mental, emotional, and psychological differences between people."

- Stephen Covey

Winning the Pitch requires a winning pitch team. But who should be on the team? How many people, and in what roles? If your team is too big, you can overwhelm the client.

> I once attended a pitch where our team had 12 attendees. We had a full pitch team, managers, and others 'just in case'. We were going to show our great interest in the business. I cannot say we were well-prepared; perhaps we were attempting to make up in quantity what we lacked in quality. On the big day, our prospect came with two others. 12 to 3. Needless to say, it was an uncomfortable meeting. I am sure the prospect was wondering if all these people didn't have something better to do (and how much cost they added to our proposal).

There are clearly problems if the team is too large. However, if the pitch team is too small, you risk creating the impression that the opportunity is not important. To determine the best number, look into the audience and its interests. Make sure your team can handle the breadth and depth of the issues which are likely to arise. If their finance director is attending, ensure you have appropriate financial expertise available. If detailed technical discussions are anticipated, have your technical experts on the team. In general, the higher the value of the work and the more complex, the larger the team will be.

Clients will be more comfortable with your proposal if the people they are meeting be assigned to the project. Of course this is not always possible, but many prospects will ask this question.

The following roles are important to the pitch process.

Team Leader

This person is responsible for leading the pitch. Everyone reports to the team leader for this opportunity, and he or she will be responsible for calling meetings and directing the effort. Team leaders may be the senior person, and often will be the RM or sales lead on the account — the person who has the relationship — who best knows the client. A good team leader will:

- Motivate the team by setting the direction, getting people excited, playing down disappointments, and being innovative.

- Coordinate and ensure that everything is on target, that each member of the team has the help they need, and that each aspect of the pitch fits into the overall plan.

Pitch Coordinator

This person ensures that the left hand knows what the right hand is doing. He or she gets all the participants to the meetings. This person is the eyes and ears of the team leader. A team needs to stay focused and make tough decisions. The pitch coordinator keeps track of the small but important things. This person is responsible for doing and/or delegating the back office jobs, such as:

- Preparing materials
- Doing the administration and logistics
- Managing equipment, technology, and materials on the day of the pitch
- Handling logistics
- Doing the follow-up

Team Members

The best pitch teams have a good mix of individuals: visionary, approachable, analytical, business-driven, process-driven, and skilled at working with people. A well-coordinated team with a blend of styles will help you get the best results before, during, and after the pitch.

Senior Management

When pitching for a high-value account, you may want to include your top executives. Senior management team members can impress the client, and their presence can create positive results. But their presence could also result in the client expecting that person to remain involved in the account once you have won it.

Also, be careful of senior management "stealing the show," or making promises you cannot keep. Senior management *must* be seen as a part of the team. It's up to the team leader to ensure the managers know the role and stick to it.

Summary

- The right number of players on your team is determined by the size of the client's team, and the complexity of the opportunity
- Seek to identify and fill four key roles on your team; ensure all are aware of their role:
  o Leader
  o Coordinator
  o Members
  o Management

The Prospect's Team

"Never forget:
the secret of creating riches for oneself
is to create them for others."

- Sir John Templeton

What Keeps Them Awake At Night?

When investigating the pitch panel, or the prospect's team, do your best to understand their buying needs. Why are they issuing an RFP? What are their motivations? What's on their mind? What keeps them awake at night? The more you can understand about the prospect's desires, wants, motivations, and drivers, the better you can adapt your pitch to meet their needs — and the more likely you are to win the business.

Business relationships are built on *value*. If you offer value, you can win the business. Core business values are simple: more revenue or lower cost. These are bottom-line, hard benefits.

But also remember the other value — personal value. We don't always buy on strict parameters of cost and revenue. People are motivated by much more than these rational drivers. We buy for many reasons, and not all of them are logical. Why does the lady buy the Gucci purse? Why does the man buy a Rolex? These clearly are not 100 percent rational purchases. When a simple cloth bag or a $20 watch will suffice, it's clear that there are other factors at work.

My neighbor Ron came home last year with a beautiful, fully-appointed full-size BMW sedan. When the neighbors came around, admiring all the features: high-tech engine, adjustable, heated leather seats, beautiful sound, and built-in GPS, he smiled and acknowledged them at first. Slowly, however, he began to protest. He acknowledged the beauty and comfort; however, he explained the reason for buying was the outstanding quality and resale value. He went on to produce data supporting these purchase factors.

Though it is undoubtedly a good quality vehicle, it was clear to the neighborhood that Ron had bought the car to provide emotional needs: the need to look and feel good, perhaps the need to be envied, to be looked up to, to impress others. And, I'm sure it was clear to Ron. However, he was justifying the purchase with a rational explanation.

While we may not have bought a BMW, we all have had some shared experience with Ron. We know what it feels like to buy with emotion.

The truth is, we buy for many emotional reasons. We buy for ego and status, to look good and to feel good. We buy to impress. We buy based on fear, brand, culture, politics, past affiliations, and because the boss did so. We buy because we like one person or team over another. We buy for soft, personal benefits. People buy with emotion and justify with logic.

Most people intuitively agree when I discuss this topic, but only recently have I found research that supports it. Our understanding of the workings of the brain is growing rapidly. Today, the nerve cell networks in our brains are being mapped. This technology of *functional neuroimaging* is providing us with new ways of looking at how our emotions are programmed within the brain.

"Emotional and rational parts of the brain may be more closely intertwined than previously thought," according to Dean Shibata, assistant professor of radiology at the University of Washington. Shibata scans the brains of subjects involved in making decisions. When the decisions involve health or well-being, the subject needs to "feel" the projected emotional outcome of each choice either subconsciously or intuitively. Says Shibata, "That feeling guides you and gives you a motivation to make the best choice, often in a split second. When people make decisions that affect their own lives, they will utilize emotional parts of the brain, even though the task itself may not seem emotional."[1]

Sure, but does the product or service you are pitching affect your prospect's *life*? You bet. You are attempting to change his business life. This will often directly affect his personal life (e.g., time with family, promotions, etc.). We know that change often brings some sense of loss — loss of the old, comfortable ways. Organizational change also brings stress due to job change and uncertainty. Therefore, *expect* emotions to enter the decision.

The Primitive Brain

Whether we want to admit it or not, we still are strongly driven by the "primitive" or "reptilian" brain — that core of the brain which developed first, and is responsible for survival. It makes quick decisions to keep us secure. When the tiger roams too close to the tribe on the savannah, there is no time to think, procrastinate, or deliberate. Don't think. Decide. Move. Now! The primitive brain acts quickly. Appealing to your prospect's primitive brain will help you get quicker decisions.

In seeking survival, the primitive brain is driven by emotion and simple visual stimuli. It deals with the concrete, not the abstract. Do you get emotional when it comes to your survival? Of course you do. What do you get emotional about? You get emotional about things you *value*, and things that *hurt* you.

Consider the above as fundamental knowledge — first principles — when Pitching to Win. The decision will not be completely rational. While the rational cortex is analyzing away, the prospect's primitive brain will react to the pitch emotionally as he "feels" the projected emotional outcome of the choice you are proposing. So *sell to the primitive brain*: use emotion, simple visuals, and concrete examples. Avoid technical details, specifications, and jargon as much as you posssibly can. *Don't make them think.*

Speak the Language

Every company has its own terminology and its own language. I remember listening in on a group during a break in training at a major technology client. I knew a few of the buzzwords, abbreviations, and acronyms. But the group could have been speaking Arabic. I was lost in the conversation. It was in English, but it was a very specific dialect. Every company has a specific language.

Listen carefully to the words your prospect uses, and incorporate this exact wording in your pitch. When you "speak the language," you will be more readily accepted. You will build a subtle connection between your team and the prospect. For example, your prospect may use *revenue* instead of *income, clients* rather than *customers*, and *RMs* rather than *sales people*. You don't have to know all the acronyms, but be attuned to the language of the buyer, and you'll immediately be seen more as an insider and build rapport.

Buying Influence Types

To understand how the client buys, start by understanding the roles your different contacts play in the sales process. Any deal of complexity will involve these Buying Influence Types. Your job is to identify them and to ensure their buying needs are met. Note that some buyers may fill multiple roles. Also note that these are specific to each pitch — the roles and influence change for different deals. I suggest you look for four Buying Influence Types.

Economic Buyer (EB): The EB gives final approval to a purchase. There is generally only one per deal (could be a committee or board). The EB:

- Controls expenditure of funds

- Has discretionary use of resources
- Can say yes when everyone else says no (and vice-versa)
- Is the M.A.N.: has Money, Authority, and Need

The EB is looking for consensus in employing results-oriented solutions which deliver practical business results.

Experience shows that, in every complex deal, finding the Economic Buyer is critical. You may not see this person regularly, but it's important to be aware of who he is because of his power. How can you find the EB?

- Ask the suspected EB directly
- Ask your Coach
- Ask all in the deal: what is the decision-making process for this deal?
- If you are blocked from meeting the EB, show the "blocker" a way to win — find his buying need
- Go around or go along with the blocker

Remember, the EB is human, like us all, and is driven by similar needs and wants.

Technical Buyer (TB): The TB checks fit-for-purpose and screens out. The TB:

- Judges measurable aspects (checks the box)
- Is the gatekeeper
- Cannot give final approval
- Can veto based on specs or technicalities

The TB is looking to meet maintenance and design specs, support, and quality and safety concerns. This user wants data to support technically proven solutions. When meeting the TB, your job is to convince him that your specifications match his needs.

User Buyer (UB): The UB judges impact on job performance. The UB:

- Will use, or supervise people using, your product or service
- Is a direct link between users' success and your success

The UB will focus on the job to be done. This buying influence will be checking productivity, user-friendliness, training, and performance standards. This buyer often wants no surprises, and needs to make the job simple and easier for the team to meet productivity objectives.

Coach: The Coach acts as a guide for this pitch.

- Helps navigate the politics and other influences in the buyer
- May stand up for your solution

The Coach is your key helper in the prospect's organization. An effective Coach will be seen as credible and influential in the buying organization. The coach is working for your success on this pitch. The successful pitch team will proactively develop at least one coach for a pitch of any complexity.

Years ago, I was selling a complex software and hardware solution into a remote location in the Middle East. The client, a technically demanding Japanese team, was very unfamiliar with my solution. They also were risk-averse, and prone to stick with the tried-and-true solution – which mine certainly was not.

The only way to win them over was to develop a coach. Hirokawa-san turned out to be ideal. Young and idealistic, but savvy and respected, he was a key member of the technical evaluation group. We developed good rapport from the beginning, discussing the challenges of living and working remotely, implementing new solutions, and operating through the bureaucratic system. While he demanded strict specifications, technical rigor, and competitive pricing, he clearly championed my team's solution in client meetings.

One day during a meeting, he quickly got up from his desk, and asked me to follow him into a small storeroom. He surreptitiously produced a computer printout – a printout that showed the budget for the system in some detail. Even though it was hot, and the light was dim, I quickly memorized the relevant facts and numbers. We won that deal – the first of its kind in the region. We won because I had a good coach. That coach went on to be a friend.

For all buying influences, your job is to determine buying needs. Learn how to help them win. Get to know their drivers and needs. Give them both bottom-line and personal benefits. When you effectively meet both personal and business needs, you have a much better chance of winning.

Buyer Degree of Influence

Now, rank your buyers by *degree of influence* on a simple Low, Medium, and High scale, depending upon how strongly they will affect the decision. Factors affecting the degree of influence of any given person include organizational impact, level of expertise, buyer personal priorities, and internal politics.

Buyer Ratings

This is a simple scale for rating how the buyer feels about your solution.

+5   Enthusiastic Advocate

+4   Strongly Supportive

+3   Supportive

+2   Interested

+1   Will Go Along

-1   Probably Won't Resist

-2   Uninterested

-3   Negative

-4   Strong for Competition

-5   Antagonistic, Anti-Sponsor

Note there is no zero. Take a stand with all buying influence types![2]

Putting It Together: The Power Map

The Power Structure shows the buyers graphically on the client's team for this pitch. It is not an organizational chart, but a power chart. It is a planning and communication tool to help your team — and any relevant outsiders — understand the buyers' roles. You can use this tool along with the checklists given previously to gather intelligence on competition, products, and the client organization's buying preferences and processes. When complete and accurate, the Power Map clearly shows both the key players in the pitch and who you need to contact to get more information.

Name / Title		
Type	**Influence Level**	**Rating**

Building Blocks for the Power Map

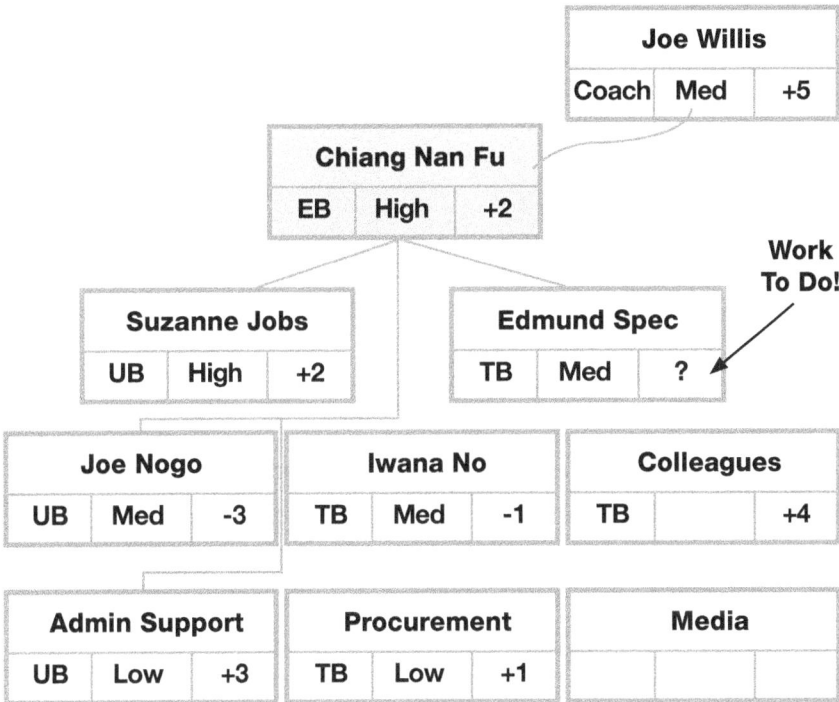

Joe Willis		
Coach	Med	+5

Chiang Nan Fu		
EB	High	+2

Work To Do!

Suzanne Jobs		
UB	High	+2

Edmund Spec		
TB	Med	?

Joe Nogo		
UB	Med	-3

Iwana No		
TB	Med	-1

Colleagues		
TB		+4

Admin Support		
UB	Low	+3

Procurement		
TB	Low	+1

Media		

The Power Map shows the key buyers and
is a useful communication tool.

In the Power Map above, the Coach (Joe), the Technical Buyer
(Edmund), and the key User Buyer (Suzanne), influence the
Economic Buyer (Chiang). Other buying influences are ranked lower
(but still are important). Note that the Buyer Rating for Edmund
Spec is unknown. This is a key unknown, and your job is to put a
rating in the box. Don't assume! Meet with this key influence and
determine how he feels about your product or solution.

Also note that some of the other key buyers' ratings may be able to be raised with a meeting. Perhaps Joe simply needs to meet with your usability or user interface expert to move his rating into a positive range. It may be that Iwana needs more technical information. That is your job in the complex sale.

In my workshops, I regularly ask how many people *really* count in a given complex pitch. The answers are very few: usually three to six people are key for any given deal. Knowing this should be reassuring; you don't have to cover dozens of influences. Focus on those with a direct impact on this pitch at this time.

Summary

- The better you understand the prospect's buying needs, the better you can meet them

- We buy with emotion and justify with logic

- We are emotional about things we value, and things that can hurt us

- The Power Map is a planning and communication tool to help you and your team understand the prospect's buying influences

The Competition

"Opportunities are never lost; someone will take the one you miss."

- Author Unknown

Keep in mind that assessing the competition is an ongoing process. For a given pitch, you should be able to draw upon the corporate memory, understanding the previous strengths and strategies of a competitor. Don't make the mistake of thinking you understand the competition just because you see them at trade shows, socially, or in other settings. Below is a profile form, the answers to which will allow your team to form a detailed analysis of your game plan vis-à-vis the competition. It allows you to answer the four critical questions:

- What is the competitor doing?
- What is the competitor capable of doing?
- What will the competitor do going forward?
- What should we do?

COMPETITOR PROFILE FORM
Competitor's name:
Competitor's product/service
Market share/trend
Estimated sales volume
Current priorities
Known objectives
Strengths
Weaknesses
Advantages (over us)
Disadvantages (versus us)
Cash position
Cost position
Profit picture
Strategy (for the short term)
Strategy (for the long term)
Suggested counterstrategy

"If you know the enemy and know yourself you need not fear the results of a hundred battles."

- Sun Tzu

Form an internal intelligence-gathering unit to gather information on your primary competitors. The better you know the competitor's products and services, the better you can offset their plans. The intelligence network includes: R&D and product people who study competitors' product and service designs and costs; the sales staff who pick up information from customers; purchasing personnel who collect data from suppliers; and the public relations staff who cultivate sources in the industry.

To have a meaningful competitive analysis, a company has to look at and analyze all the following key factors affecting competition.

1. There are six threats that affect competition in any industry: bargaining power of buyers, bargaining power of suppliers,

threat of potential new entrants into the market, threat
of substitute products or services, threat of government
intervention, and rivalry between companies within a segment
of an industry.

When you review these six threats, ask yourself: At what stage
in the industry's life cycle is your company? Is it emerging,
growing, or maturing? Is it a fragmented industry? If it's an
emerging industry, the threat of potential new entrants and
threat of substitute products may impact your company more
severely than the other four. Today, for example, if you're in
banking, the threat of government intervention may be your
biggest concern.

2. Shifting market forces is one of the more difficult areas
    to analyze and probably the most important. If you can
    anticipate market shifts, you can gain a head start by
    exploiting new trends. Market shifts may be triggered by
    demographic changes, government regulation, technological
    innovation, or new needs in the market.

    Attempt to understand what forces are shifting now, what
    shifted in the past, and what may shift in the future. Identify
    the most likely events that can happen in your industry and
    how they would affect the market forces.

3. Your industry profile is important. Look at your industry in
    total. Identify the major players and the industry segments
    they cover, and decide where in the industry's life cycle you
    belong. Look for openings in your industry that are not being
    addressed, and act decisively and fast without attracting too
    much attention.

Competitor Intelligence Checklist

As we studied in college, you can never know enough. The price of
perfect information is infinite. To have the best chance of winning
a pitch, there are certain things you must know, some things you
should know, and some things you would like to know about the
competition, the product, and the client. The following checklist is

based upon one used by a Fortune 500 company. Use it to examine some of the elements of competitor intelligence. Then you can rate this information, and develop an appropriate course of action.

What You Need to Know about the Competition

1. **What is the competitor's financial standing? Is it so precarious that the competitor will sell at prices that just pay operating costs?**

   ☐ Must know   ☐ Should know   ☐ Would like to know

   Your evaluation:_____

   ☐ Definite advantage   ☐ Possible advantage
   ☐ Possible disadvantage   ☐ Definite disadvantage

   Possible effect on pitch:_____

   Proposed action:_____

2. **What it the competitor's bargaining position? Are its products and services highly sought after?**

   ☐ Must know   ☐ Should know   ☐ Would like to know

   Your evaluation:_____

   ☐ Definite advantage   ☐ Possible advantage
   ☐ Possible disadvantage   ☐ Definite disadvantage

   Possible effect on pitch:_____

   Proposed action:_____

3. **Can it afford to give the service you can give? Can it provide better service than you can?**

   ☐ Must know   ☐ Should know   ☐ Would like to know

   Your evaluation:_____

   ☐ Definite advantage   ☐ Possible advantage
   ☐ Possible disadvantage   ☐ Definite disadvantage

   Possible effect on pitch:_____

   Proposed action:_____

---

4. **What are its selling practices? What strategies and tactics is it known to pursue habitually?**

    ☐ Must know   ☐ Should know   ☐ Would like to know

    Your evaluation:_____

    ☐ Definite advantage   ☐ Possible advantage

    ☐ Possible disadvantage   ☐ Definite disadvantage

    Possible effect on pitch:_____

    Proposed action:_____

5. **Who, specifically, is the competition? Who actually calls on the client?**

    ☐ Must know   ☐ Should know   ☐ Would like to know

    Your evaluation:_____

    ☐ Definite advantage   ☐ Possible advantage

    ☐ Possible disadvantage   ☐ Definite disadvantage

    Possible effect on pitch:_____

    Proposed action:_____

6. **Does your competition sell to your client?**

    ☐ Must know   ☐ Should know   ☐ Would like to know

    Your evaluation:_____

    ☐ Definite advantage   ☐ Possible advantage

    ☐ Possible disadvantage   ☐ Definite disadvantage

    Possible effect on pitch:_____

    Proposed action:_____

7. **Is your customer located in the same city as your competition? Will this be used as a selling advantage?**

☐ Must know ☐ Should know ☐ Would like to know

Your evaluation:_____

☐ Definite advantage ☐ Possible advantage

☐ Possible disadvantage ☐ Definite disadvantage

Possible effect on pitch:_____

Proposed action:_____

8. **Do any personal relationships exist between members of your competitor's organization and the client?**

☐ Must know ☐ Should know ☐ Would like to know

Your evaluation:_____

☐ Definite advantage ☐ Possible advantage

☐ Possible disadvantage ☐ Definite disadvantage

Possible effect on pitch:_____

Proposed action:_____

9. **Do your competitor and your customer have social, fraternal, ethnic, trade, or financial relationships?**

☐ Must know ☐ Should know ☐ Would like to know

Your evaluation:_____

☐ Definite advantage ☐ Possible advantage

☐ Possible disadvantage ☐ Definite disadvantage

Possible effect on pitch:_____

Proposed action:_____

10. Did your competitor win the last bid from this customer? Why?

☐ Must know   ☐ Should know ☐ Would like to know

Your evaluation:_____

☐ Definite advantage   ☐ Possible advantage

☐ Possible disadvantage ☐ Definite disadvantage

Possible effect on pitch:_____

Proposed action:_____

11. Does your competitor have access to information about your customer that is not available to you?

☐ Must know   ☐ Should know ☐ Would like to know

Your evaluation:_____

☐ Definite advantage   ☐ Possible advantage

☐ Possible disadvantage ☐ Definite disadvantage

Possible effect on pitch:_____

Proposed action:_____

12. Does your competitor's organization permit it to operate more rapidly than you can?

☐ Must know   ☐ Should know ☐ Would like to know

Your evaluation:_____

☐ Definite advantage   ☐ Possible advantage

☐ Possible disadvantage ☐ Definite disadvantage

Possible effect on pitch:_____

Proposed action:_____

13. Can the competitor see the customer more often than you?

☐ Must know ☐ Should know ☐ Would like to know

Your evaluation:_____

☐ Definite advantage ☐ Possible advantage

☐ Possible disadvantage ☐ Definite disadvantage

Possible effect on pitch:_____

Proposed action:_____

14. What marketing strengths and weaknesses does it have?

☐ Must know ☐ Should know ☐ Would like to know

Your evaluation:_____

☐ Definite advantage ☐ Possible advantage

☐ Possible disadvantage ☐ Definite disadvantage

Possible effect on pitch:_____

Proposed action:_____

15. Who are your competitor's key customers? Will they influence this customer? In what way?

☐ Must know ☐ Should know ☐ Would like to know

Your evaluation:_____

☐ Definite advantage ☐ Possible advantage

☐ Possible disadvantage ☐ Definite disadvantage

Possible effect on pitch:_____

Proposed action:_____

Summary

- Use a Competitor Profile Form to better understand the six threats affecting your industry

- A Competitor Checklist is a useful tool for gaining specific details of the competition

Create the Story

Set Objectives

"If you don't know where you are going, you will probably end up somewhere else."

- Lawrence J. Peter

The ultimate objective is to win the business. Depending upon your industry, product, and sales cycle, you are unlikely to win the business during the first or second meeting. The overall pitch process usually requires a series of meetings and presentations, as you navigate the client organization.

Therefore, you need to set clear objectives for *each* client contact — whether that contact is a meeting, phone call, or presentation. If you don't have a valid business objective, then that visit is a social call. I'm not saying that there isn't a place for social calls; simply that they may not contribute to your objective or shorten your sales cycle. Most people are not paid for social calls.

For example, if you know that the client will be creating the short list of potential vendors after the first presentation, your realistic objective would be to get on the short list. In this case, winning the business is not a valid objective for this call. Setting realistic objectives will help ensure your message is relevant for the client at this point in the sales cycle.

Ultimate Objective Steps

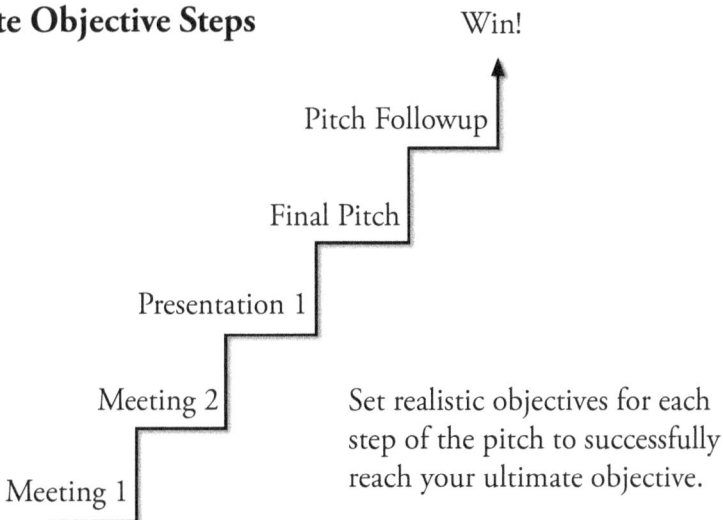

Win!

Pitch Followup

Final Pitch

Presentation 1

Meeting 2

Meeting 1

Set realistic objectives for each step of the pitch to successfully reach your ultimate objective.

Have you ever been to a presentation and, after it was over, asked yourself, "What was that all about?" I suspect most of us have had this experience. It's a sure bet the presenter didn't set her objectives, and therefore the audience is left guessing as to the desired outcome of the talk. Stephen Covey, in *Seven Habits of Highly Effective People,* says "Begin with the end in mind." That's good advice whether you are planning a business strategy, setting personal goals, or setting objectives for a pitch. Determine early in the process what you want from the pitch.

Setting objectives sounds easy. However, we find most pitch teams set unclear or unrealistic objectives. Realizing where you are in the process will help. So how do you make the objective clear? Follow a straightforward three-step process.

I suggest you start with the *why* question. Ask why it's important to the prospect, why he should attend the pitch, why he should care. Asking *why* gets deeper than the rational, and penetrates to the primitive brain — it gets to the root of the emotional need to buy. Go beyond the simple explanations like "it's their job, and they have to attend." If you can dig a bit deeper, you can start to uncover much more compelling motivations — for them and for you.

Give Them a WIIFM

It may sound harsh, but people are focused mainly on themselves. We all are tuned to the #1 radio station WIIFM (What's In It For Me?). As stated before, the prospect doesn't care about you except with regards to what you can do to help him or her. It's human nature and basic to survival.

So give them a WIIFM! Answer the question *What's in it for me?* from the *prospect's* perspective. Then you will get their attention — and find yourself with an open, willing audience. Constantly ask the question in any persuasive situation and you will keep your pitch focused where it needs to be: *on the prospect.* Generally, there is one overarching WIIFM which unites the pitch for a given prospect and situation. For example, a software company selling integration is pitching at the highest level to the WIIFM of simplicity, less maintenance, and less potential downtime.

In addition to these overarching WIIFMs, there are any number of specific but still significant audience benefits in any pitch. A *benefit* is something of value to the audience. Whenever you state a fact or idea, link it to a specific benefit. Here are some examples of how to do it:

- What does this mean to you? (followed by explanation)
- This is important in your case because… (followed by explanation)
- Why am I saying this?
- So what this does for you is…(what?).
- So what?
- Who cares?
- And…? (with explanation).

So, for example, when you find yourself touting your global team, ask, "So what? Does the prospect care?" You may be surprised at how often the answer is a resounding *no*. Asking the above questions immediately establishes relevance. It helps you create relevant benefits. *Why* would the prospect care in his situation or given her constraints?

Winning Pitch presenters ask the WIIFM question for any statements made about themselves, their company, and their product or service. Spell out the specific benefits clearly and precisely.

Sometimes people feel this is unnecessary. Many sales people I work with make the assumption that the prospect will automatically *get* the WIIFM. I encourage you to be very clear about the benefits. You don't know the audience's frame of mind, their attention level, or their ability to see the issue the way you do. Always connect the feature to the benefit, even if it's obvious to you. *Don't make them think*. When you spell it out clearly, in your buyer's language, your persuasive ability can only increase. Your audience will thank you for being clear. You manage the discussion, and instill confidence in your story.

Three A's

The second step, once you have a clear overarching *why*, is to ask *what*. Ask, "What is the purpose of the talk?" It will most likely be one of the *Three A's*:

- Increase *Awareness*
- Modify *Attitude*
- Persuade to *Action*

All of these A's are valid statements of purpose. They are necessary, but not sufficient. The purpose — the *what* — is where most presenters start and stop. "I'm here to inform you about our product." That one is a guaranteed turn-off. I recommend taking it a step further. There is more to the Winning Pitch objective-setting process — a call to action.

Many speakers, when asked for an objective, state something like, "to educate the client about our product," or "to inform them about our business." If you are thinking this is a viable objective, simply put yourself in the audience's place. Do you want to go to a meeting, drink the bad coffee, and eat the rubber chicken, to be educated and informed? I doubt it. Objectives of this type are almost guaranteed to create information overload and bored audiences.

Recently, Thomas — a senior sales executive client — would not back down on his objective, "To inform them about our new product." I pushed hard over a couple of meetings to make the objective more action-oriented, but to no avail. Finally, on the third meeting, he surprised me with a reworked objective: "To persuade them our product is the best in its field, and get the decision-maker's approval." Now that was a much more interesting objective, and one from which he was able to build a strong, compelling pitch. When I asked Thomas what caused him to change, he sheepishly stated he came at last to the realization that the previous objective was all about his company — not the prospect — and would lead to a one-way, boring presentation which was likely to fall short of what he really wanted to accomplish.

What Do You Want?

> *"The ultimate aim of all speaking is action."*
> *- Ralph Waldo Emerson*

Thirdly, ask about *outcome*. When your purpose is achieved — when changes occur in the audience's Awareness, Attitude, and Action — what will result? What do you want the audience to *think, feel, or do* differently at the end of the pitch? Note that these three words involve the head, the heart, and the body. They cover the logical, the emotional, and the physical. They affect the primitive brain. This is the key step, and it's a step few people really take.

You are not there simply to inform them or to educate them. Setting these as objectives leads to dull, lifeless presentations. Unless you actually *change* something with your presentation, unless your listeners are different after the presentation — unless you have had an *effect* on them, you haven't been *effective*! *Clearly* identify the outcome. If you cannot, then stop. You have no audience benefits. They won't care. Go back to step 2 and reexamine the purpose.

Now a reality test: again, given the step in the pitch process, the sales cycle, and the current environment and relationship, ask yourself: "Is this outcome achievable?"

State your objective simply and succinctly. You may have two objectives (or maybe three, but no more). State each one in a simple, actionable sentence. Examples might be: "Get a meeting with the decision-maker within 10 days" or "Make the short list of three providers."

The 1-2-3-Step Objective-Setting Process:

1. Why? Why should they care?
2. What? What is the purpose: Awareness, Attitude, and/or Action?
3. Outcome? What do I want them to *think, feel, or do*?

When you complete this 1-2-3-Step Objective-Setting Process, you already have two major portions of the pitch completed: the Benefits and the Close (we will come to these later). I strongly encourage clients to write their objectives down clearly, tape them on their desk, send them by e-mail, and prominently display them on the team's intranet; and ensure the entire pitch team buys into the objectives and will follow them as they develop their messages.

Summary

- Pitching is a process. Create an objective for every meeting in the process.

- Business meetings have a clear objective, or they are social calls.

The 1-2-3-Step Objective-Setting process is:

1. Give them a WIIFM!

2. Define the purpose: Increase *Awareness*, modify *Attitude*, and/or persuade to *Action*

3. Clearly state your objective: What do you want them to do, think, or feel as a result of the presentation?

Develop the Message

"The way we communicate with others and with ourselves ultimately determines the quality of our lives."

- Anthony Robbins

Stop Killing People

How many times have you sat through a meeting trying to stay awake, feeling like the people in the picture above? You were dying. So was the presenter. All are victims of PowerPoint and Data Dumps.

Creating a powerful pitch requires a clear story. Too many pitches are simply Data Dumps — they overflow with facts, data, and logic, all poured out without structure or purpose. Your objective will clarify your purpose. But what about the structure? How do you tell them what they need to know without boring them with too much detail or subjecting them to a Data Dump?

This working day, about 30 million people will deliver a PowerPoint presentation. That means millions of people right now are *dying* — killed by the growing disease, "Death by PowerPoint"! Both onstage and in the audience, people are being subjected to all varieties of information overload from PowerPoint and Data Dump. In this chapter we will examine how you can stop the carnage.

Message development is both an art and a science. The art is in the story: what's included, why we focus upon certain aspects, and how we put our pitch together so it's creative, interesting, and engaging. The science is in being clear regarding objectives, grabbers, transitions, summaries, and the flow — the logical sequence of concepts — all the organizational aspects of the story.

Start Right with the Right Brain

If you are like most business people, you are successful because you get things done rapidly, you recycle, you delegate, and you multitask. These skills are efficient, but they are in direct opposition to those needed to develop powerful presentations.

Calling on these skills when building a pitch, you quickly cobble together a set of slides from previous presentations or a corporate standard deck, and/or you delegate the slides to a PA or a graphic specialist. Next, you spend a good bit of time aimlessly shuffling the slides around until you feel they are beginning to make sense. During this phase, you may create some new ones, add a few from a previous presentation, or get some from a colleague. You think about what you will say about each slide. At some point, you convince yourself that this set of slides, with a few appropriate comments, will become an engaging presentation. Unfortunately, rather than engaging and motivating the audience, these types of presentations become just another in a series of boring "Death by PowerPoint" exercises. The outcome is repeated far too often: the audience tolerates them — barely — and you decide you're just "not a good speaker."

Clearly the skills involved in creating an engaging presentation differ from the skills you have used to become a successful executive. Building a presentation is a *creative* process. According to many scientists, the left and right halves of the brain are responsible for different forms of reasoning. The left side controls logical concepts, such as mathematical and linear functions. The right side, in contrast, deals more with creative concepts. It's more holistic, and is essentially nonlinear, more expansive, and imaginative.

The right side creates and builds up; the left side drills down and focuses. Both are important in developing a pitch; however, developing a pitch first with left-brain considerations such as logic, sequence, slide design, and bullet points is not effective. It leads to a boring death. To create a powerful pitch, start with the art — and that means using the right brain. To develop a story, one method is to follow the stream of consciousness and capture the results using brainstorming.

Rules for Brainstorming

- Have one minute of quiet time before starting.
- Organize the group around the flip chart.
- Nominate a scribe and a facilitator.
- Set a time limit.
- One person calls out an idea for what should go into the pitch (e.g., Our Products).
- Rotate around the group so that each member gives his or her input.
- Allow a member to pass if they cannot contribute on their turn (limit this to 2 passes per person).
- Free-wheel around the group if input begins to slow down.
- The scribe must not edit.
- Ideas *must not be judged* or criticized.
- No thinking about structure, hierarchy, or sequence.
- Be creative; build on other ideas.
- All ideas will be captured.

Done properly, the flip chart will have a large number of items; some clear, some unclear; some important, others less so. The point is that the entire group will be able to see all the elements of your pitch, laid out in clear view.

Now you can start organizing this relative mess into a clearly focused presentation using a technique known as clustering. Clustering is an ancient technique wherein you examine the output of the brainstorm and, using different colored markers, begin to identify links and connections. You start to see common themes and ideas emerging from the relative chaos of the brainstorming session. You may move concepts around; you likely will see new connections emerging that you never would have been aware of had you started in the common, left-brained, sequenced approach. Having held back your left brain, you now apply it where it's best. You will eliminate some ideas. Others will be clarified and amplified. When you have a clustered set of ideas created in this manner, you are well on your way to an engaging presentation. Only after you have this plan, should you even think about opening PowerPoint or OneNote.

"There's just something about paper and pen in sketching out rough ideas in the 'analog world' in the early stages that seems to lead to more clarity and better, more creative results when we finally get down to representing our ideas digitally," says Garr Reynolds in Presentation Zen.[3]

The Flow

When presenting, you are the navigator. Help your audience to see where the pitch is going. Give them a map. It's important to recognize your audience does not have access to the material that is coming up, nor will it have ready reference to what you said five minutes before. Unlike the written word, the spoken word is ephemeral, and we cannot access it immediately by, "turning back in the book." Therefore, a good presenter will lay out the ideas in a logical sequence and guide the audience through them. There are many flow structures you can choose when presenting. I always recommend starting with your objective and your audience.

Who Is This About?

The problem with pitching is that you need to sell yourself and your product or ideas. You want the prospect to know why yours is better than the others and by how much! You have a need to sell. The prospect, on the other hand, doesn't really care about you. He cares about his own problems — you only come into the picture to the extent that you can help him with his problems. He has a need to buy.

Poor sellers often fail to recognize the reality of the market. This misunderstanding of today's competitive market — and our need to sell — results in many of us presenting our case in the wrong way.

Here is what we see routinely:

1. **The opening:** Let me introduce our company and tell you about our hundred-year history, our global coverage, and all the awards we have won.

2. **The product:** These are the data and greatly detailed workings that enable us to offer this great list of features.

3. **The offer:** This is what it will cost you and when we can deliver.

The whole pitch is about the supplier. It's all about us! The potential buyer hardly gets a look in. It's a bit like going out to dinner with proud new parents. You can appreciate the miracle, but the conversation can get very one-sided and boring!

The team who can put themselves in the buyer's shoes understands this reaction and empathizes with the selfishness. Much of what we have to say may be the same, but the words are couched in terms that look at the world from the *buyer's* perspective — something like this:

1. **The opening:** This is your world and your problem; we recognize its uniqueness and challenge, and we can help.

2. **The offer:** These are the benefits we can contribute and how they will help you. This is what these benefits will cost.

3. **The advantage:** This is who we are and how we can help you. We are credible. Here is relevant evidence of our track record and the benefits it offers to you. This is our competitive advantage and how it addresses your agenda.

This pitch is about the buyer; not the seller. It uses the language of the buyer. As a potential customer, do you want to listen to people talk about themselves or about you? Ask yourself, do you like *buy* or to *be sold to*?

We will be looking in more detail at how to flow presentations, but these two contrasting examples should serve to illustrate the difference that *focusing on me* vs. *focusing on you* can make.

The Map: Flow

There are a number of proven techniques for organizing ideas in a logical sequence to create a convincing presentation. In this section, we examine some of the most common techniques.

Context/Concept/Form

The Granddaddy of many presentation techniques, this broadly applicable flow starts by setting the context. What it is that you perceive in the macro environment that you will discuss? What is the situation, issue, or problem? Then comes the concept: what is our thinking, approach, or solution to the problem? Perhaps this is the strategy — a response to the context. Finally the form: how we will execute the solution? This may be the details or the tactics we propose, and will include the benefits to the prospect.

Chronological

This is a classic form of corporate presentation. This organizes clusters of ideas in a time sequence, reflecting events as they have occurred or will occur.

Feature/Benefit/Evidence

This is a common pitching structure. The agenda items are organized around the features of the product or service and the benefits that the user will receive. Proof in the form of relevant evidence makes the pitch stronger.

Now/Be/How

A specific example of Context/Concept/Form, this structure takes the client on a journey. It's useful for presenting where you are *now*, where you want to *be* in the future, and *how* you are going to take them there.

Problem/Options/Solution

Another specific example of Context/Concept/Form, this is useful for presenting a recommendation for the best way to resolve an issue or problem.

Advantages/Disadvantages/Recommendations

This structure helps the audience examine and make decisions before determining a course of action.

Situation/Action/Results/Testimonials

This one is used when delivering a case study on a project, business initiative, or situation. It clearly states the results achieved by the client, and can include quotes or comments in support of the benefits.

Requirements/Solution/Implementation

This is the structure discussed in the opening of this section. Your background work and status in the pitch process will determine what agenda items to emphasize.

Compare/Contrast/Recommendations

This allows you to compare your solution or company with others. How do you stack up? What is your distinctive advantage or unique value? Choose this option with caution. Be careful about offending someone who may favor the other company. However, it may be very strong when comparing to the current (status quo) situation; for example, when pitching a new automated system. Use it only when you know your client and the current status well.

Which Flow?

When selecting a flow structure, consider the following factors:

- Your style — which flow *feels* right to your team? Experiment.
- The audience — what is their primary interest? The best structure is buyer-focused and meets audience needs. Keep it buyer-focused.

There is no "right" flow structure. There is some art here. Find a flow which "sounds right" or "feels right" for your team and the situation. I once worked for two full hours with an executive simply getting the flow right. We didn't do anything but anticipate how the talk would go. We spoke about the audience and how they would react to a given story or video — how they would feel. We didn't look at PowerPoint slides except on paper to see where they would best fit. Comfort with the flow is a prerequisite to a powerful pitch.

You First

If you go back to first principles — survival, "what's in it for me?" — you can uncover another great way to speak the language of the buyer. Psychologists tell us that the primitive brain moves toward pleasure and away from pain. For many people, thinking is painful. So *don't make them think*; do the thinking for them. Translate everything you can into the other person's terms by starting as many sentences as possible with the powerful word *you*. Putting *you* first gets a better response. It engages the listener and creates ownership; it "puts the ball in the listener's court."

As a simple example, when a prospect asks a question, we often respond, "That's a good question." Not bad. Now try putting yourself in the shoes of the person who hears, "*You've* asked a good question." It's a subtle but powerful difference.

Winning Pitch professionals employ this technique to keep the focus where it should be — on the prospect. What is the subject of the statement, "The system allows you to…"? Right: it's about the system. Instead, make the buyer the subject, by saying, "You can see how the system allows you to…" Good communicators convince prospects by relating to them with *you* first. Rather than telling them, "We will show you this," persuasive professionals create ownership with "You will see this." Create anticipation with "What if you could…". You can even share a sense of accomplishment. Instead of saying, "The result will be…" share the results with, "You'll see the result when…"

> **The prospect thinks *me*, so create ownership by using *you* first.**

Stories

"They may forget what you said, but they will never forget how you made them feel."

- Unknown

Do you remember stories? Most of us know the Christmas story, the classic Grimms children's stories, or the stories of great struggles depicted in movies such as Star Wars and Titanic. As a species, humans have been passing down stories and writing on cave walls for millennia. We are hard-wired to think in stories and pictures. We have had quarterly business reviews and formal pitches for about 100 years, and PowerPoint for only 25. Why is it then that most pitch teams insist on breaking out the numbers, grabbing PowerPoint, and spinning a left-brained, logical pitch as soon as the opportunity arises?

Forgetting — and Remembering

Perhaps it's because we have forgotten. We have forgotten the magic of the Christmas story, related to us by our grandfather as we gathered in the family room. We've forgotten the impact of the family stories we heard as children, and the ghost stories that interfered with our young sleep while at scout camp. While we may have forgotten the magic, we have not forgotten the stories, and that's the point. We remember stories. Think back to the past few presentations you've attended. It's a very good bet you don't remember the 15th slide, but you do remember the participant who told a good and relevant story, and you probably remember it well. Stories arouse and engage audience interest.

Storytelling in Business

Let's clear up two misperceptions that many business people harbor regarding storytelling. First, it's not just about entertainment. The use of a story to delight, challenge, instruct, and make a point has been with us for thousands of years. Heroes and villains, damsels in distress, and witches and warlocks all have been used around the community campfire to reinforce values — to lead to action. Stories serve the same purpose today. Relevant stories are a very powerful tool to motivate, to challenge, to make a point, and to illustrate a principle.

The second misconception that some business people seem to have is that the storyteller is a spinner of yarns, and is in some way in conflict with authenticity. The image of the theater has somehow reinforced this misperception. The real storyteller is principled and in complete harmony with the truth of the story. The real storyteller is targeting the heart, not just the head. In order for the audience to open the heart, it needs to be shown the storyteller also has a heart, and is humanly vulnerable in some way. Authenticity is the best way. Words which are presented in a way that engages the senses and emotions of the audience can touch them on several levels. This verbal tradition is at the center of our ability to motivate, to lead, and to sell. So how do you create a story?

Tips for Good Stories

- A good story is one that touches people in some way. The storyteller's mission is to involve the audience, and to make them interact consciously and subconsciously with the storyteller and with the story. A good story has a sense of truth and resonates with basic universal aspects of being human. It doesn't have to be profound, but a good story should move the listener to feel, think, and ponder it afterward.

- A good story has substance. Stories contain basic truths, and appeal to our innate senses. Audiences want to hear a story with direction and purpose.

- A good story will have conflict and resolution. Stories are made up of people, places, and happenings in some type of universal human drama. Strong stories usually have a well-defined main character who encounters some type of conflict and overcomes it. The action taken signifies personal growth and change and, finally, some sort of redemption. It is the believable action moving the story from beginning to middle to end that keeps the audience engaged.

- A good story creates vivid images. We want the audience to imagine images that relate to them and their experiences as the story unfolds. The use of *visual language* is important here. Paint a picture with words. Use metaphors and analogies. Appeal to all the senses with the language.

- A good story is a story that is right for your audience. Prepare properly for your audience, and then read them as you tell your story. Keep in tune with the audience.

- A good story is a story that you love and love to tell. You must love the story and believe in it to be authentic in the telling.

A story doesn't have to be long or involved. In my experience, short and pointed stories work best. If you are selling software, tell the story of the overburdened IT manager who received a call in the middle of the night and solved the problem of five clients simultaneously using your tools. If you are selling financial services, relate a story of a client who took care of his mother using the solution you are selling.

For memorable stories, ensure the moral is very clear to the listener. For some stories, you may simply state it. Then, show *relevance* to the topic. In the examples above, the relevance is quite clear. However, if you venture into more abstract stories, you may want to say, "The reason I told that story…" or "You can see how that relates to…" and then discuss your subject. Ensuring relevance — how your story applies to them, to the topic, to the product — is the key to ensuring the audience sees its importance and remembers it.

Steve Jobs is a premiere pitchman — possibly the best in our time. He uses the metaphor that a presentation is a classic story, and he sprinkles stories liberally throughout his pitches. One of his most famous talks, however, is not a product pitch. It is a different type of pitch: a commencement speech to Stanford University graduates in 2005. The pitch to the grads is to *stay hungry, stay foolish*. This speech has become an Internet sensation, far more popular on YouTube than addresses by Oprah Winfrey or J. K. Rowling. I urge you to read and watch it on the Stanford web site. In this address, Jobs uses many of the Pitching to Win techniques.

He starts the talk with humble introductory remarks, followed by a humorous, creative opening grabber:

> I am honored to be with you today at your commencement from one of the finest universities in the world. I never graduated from college. Truth be told, this is the closest I've ever gotten to a college graduation.

Then, he draws a map using the rule of three.

> Today I want to tell you three stories from my life. That's it. No big deal. Just three stories.

The structure of the talk is very simple: opening, three stories, and conclusion. Less is more. He tells stories of:

Connecting the dots: learning calligraphy which led to the Mac's fonts

Love and loss: about loving and then losing Apple's leadership

Death: his brush with pancreatic cancer.

Then, using this poignant story to build to his objective, he states:

> Your time is limited; so don't waste it living someone else's life. Don't be trapped by dogma — which is living the results of other people's thinking. Don't let the noise of others' opinions drown out your own inner voice.

Note the rule of threes with repetition in consecutive sentences. Great speakers have used this structure for centuries to make strong arguments. (Think of King's "I have a dream…") You can command an audience with it, too.

Jobs concludes this short talk with the following admonition:

> And most important, have the courage to follow your heart and intuition. They somehow already know what you truly want to become. Everything else is secondary….stay hungry, stay foolish.

Jobs repeated his theme several times in the short talk.

When pitching the value of stories to my clients, I'm often asked for something they can use. So I have collected several. For just one example of a great story you can use in many ways, look at the classic Acres of Diamonds.

Acres of Diamonds

The story — a true one — is told of an African farmer who heard tales about other farmers who had made millions by discovering diamond mines. These tales so excited the farmer that he could hardly wait to sell his farm and go prospecting for diamonds himself. He sold the farm and spent the rest of his life wandering the African continent searching unsuccessfully for the gleaming gems that brought such high prices on the markets of the world. Finally, worn out and in a fit of despondency, he threw himself into a river and drowned.

Meanwhile, the man who had bought his farm happened to be crossing the small stream on the property one day, when suddenly there was a bright flash of blue and red light from the stream bottom. He bent down and picked up a stone. It was a good-sized stone, and admiring it, he brought it home and put it on his fireplace mantel as an interesting curiosity.

Several weeks later a visitor picked up the stone, looked closely at it, hefted it in his hand, and nearly fainted. He asked the farmer if he knew what he'd found. When the farmer said no, that he thought it was a piece of crystal, the visitor said, "I tell you, I know a diamond when I see it. I know positively that is a diamond." The farmer had trouble believing that. He told the man that his creek was full of such stones, not all as large as the one on the mantel, but sprinkled generously throughout the creek bottom. Thus was discovered the diamond mine of Golconda, the richest on earth.

The farm which the first farmer had sold so that he might find a diamond mine turned out to be one of the most productive diamond mines on the entire African continent. The first farmer had owned, free and clear, *acres of diamonds*. But he had sold them for practically nothing, in order to look for them elsewhere. The moral is clear: if the first farmer had only taken the time to study and prepare himself to learn what diamonds looked like in their rough state, and to thoroughly explore the property he had before looking elsewhere, all of his wildest dreams would have come true.

This is a great story. It has all the elements: basic human emotions, conflict, resolution, human drama, vivid images, and a strong moral. It's memorable. The fact that it's true helps with credibility. How can you use this story when persuading? Can you inspire, motivate, and challenge using this story? There must be a dozen morals to it. (In fact, I have a client who is exploring them now.) Be creative. Sell to the heart. Use stories.

Primacy, Recency, and What's In Between

According to recent research, the average audience's attention span is about 10 minutes. In this text messaging, Twitter, and Blackberry age, if anything, our attention span seems to be getting shorter! And if that's not enough, here is another challenge for your pitch: we talk about 200 words per minute; we can listen to about 800. If we were to draw a curve of the typical audience's attention span, it would look something like the figure below.

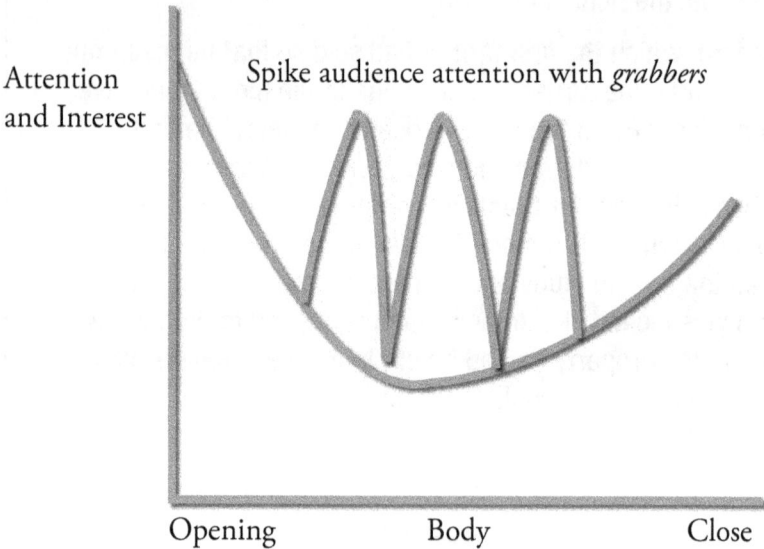

Attention and Interest — Spike audience attention with *grabbers*

Opening   Body   Close

All else being equal, a law of memory is that we remember the first things we hear (primacy) and the last things we hear (recency). Usually, the attention and interest are high at the beginning. So you have a chance to get off to a good start — if you don't blow it (see Creative Opening below). The bad news is that your audience is deep down the attention curve by the time you are talking about all your great solutions. So how do you maintain a high level of attention and interest for a talk of 30 minutes, an hour, or longer?

To grab attention and add interest, use *grabbers* during the talk. Grabbers are tools to spike audience attention. They can be many things: stories, analogies, humor, testimonials, or props. Be creative. What can you do to set your pitch apart? We react to things that are different or unusual — the primitive brain at work again. So use *change* to maintain interest. Tell a story, use a video, or change your visual aids. Do this at least every six to eight minutes. Changing presenters also will help here (if done well).

Examples of Grabbers	
Tell a relevant story	Display a relevant visual
Show an interesting video	Use a toy or prop
Use an interesting quotation	Announce a little-known fact
Post a startling statistic	Ask a relevant question
Show a demonstration	Use a puzzle

Grabbers get attention, and are remembered as they influence the emotion of the primitive brain. Jamie Oliver is now known as one of the most engaging speakers on the circuit. Oliver's passion is health and child obesity. He is a master of the grabber. Mixing startling statistics, simple graphics and engaging anecdotes with audience engagement, excitement and energy, he has made an impact on audiences globally.

In a recent award-winning TED talk, to dramatically demonstrate the amount of sugar in milk drinks consumed by the average American child, he brought out a wheelbarrow full of sugar cubes, and dumped it right out on the stage. Needless to say, the audience was engaged, and the point was vividly and memorably made. http://www.ted.com/talks/lang/eng/jamie_oliver.html

Structure: The Science

"A whole is that which has beginning, middle and end."

- Aristotle

I recently worked with a client who had a very thoughtfully prepared presentation, but didn't get to deliver it. The team was only partway through and ran out of time. The client had to leave, and didn't hear a summary. This team had not properly structured and rehearsed the pitch, and lost a key opportunity.

Have you ever sat through a talk, and when the presenter gets to a certain point, she says in mid-stream, "That's it," and everyone in the audience seems a bit surprised? How does that make you feel? To me, it feels like falling off a cliff or running into a wall. It's abrupt, unexpected, and jarring. Worse, it leaves the audience unsure of the main points and possible next steps. The speaker has missed her best chance to ensure key messages and action points come through.

Structure refers to the building blocks of the talk. You use structure to build your flow — to provide a map both for the presenters and for the audience. I recommend that teams structure each individual presentation for maximum impact, as well as structuring the overall pitch. The Pitch Presentation Planner in this section is a simple, useful tool for this purpose.

We start with the audience and the objective. The Winning Pitch team will always keep these key elements in mind.

The Opening

For most presentations, I suggest that the Opening be no more than 20 percent of the total pitch. Usually 10 percent is enough. Much more, and the audience may get lost.

Introductory Remarks

Introductory remarks serve a simple purpose: to get the audience's attention. They ensure the group is ready to listen, and they set the stage. There are a number of other things you can do during the introduction.

- Briefly introduce other presenters if you are first (recommended for a pitch)
- Give them an idea of the length, time for questions, breaks, etc.
- Tell them if and when you will distribute handouts

Deepak Chopra is a well-known author and celebrity with worldwide renown in the self-development area. In spite of this notoriety, he begins his talks and seminars with something like the following: "Thank you for being here. It is a great honor and privilege to be here with you and spend the next few hours together."

Chopra's opening is humble and appreciative of the audience. It talks about them, not him. It gives the audience praise and status.

Creative Opening

A Creative Opening is a type of Grabber meant to engage the audience's attention at the outset. It is meant to keep the initial interest high. If you don't get their attention quickly, you can easily lose them early. A Creative Opening can take many forms:

- Tell a story or anecdote
- Relate a recent news event
- Use a relevant quotation
- Show a video
- Ask the audience a question (often rhetorical)
- Get the audience to do something

Relevant Creative Openings make for a strong start and increase audience engagement, setting the stage for a good presentation. When they work, they really help your pitch. The key to making a Creative Opening work is *relevance*. Ensure you link the Creative Opening and the subject. If the story or quote is relevant to your topic, it will set the stage well. So, to ensure engagement, make good use of relevance and ensure you are clear on the link — even if you have to overtly state it.

Subject

The Subject is simply what you are there to discuss. Rather than something like "Our Plan", consider using a theme for your pitch. On a recent pitch, we brainstormed how we could tell a different story from the competition. Adding value and reducing costs both were discussed. We settled on a theme of "Adding Value to Your Business," which was a nice benefit statement, and all about the buyer. All presentations then were built to this theme, which was nicely illustrated in several ways by each presenter during the talks, with a key summary point.

Thinking in Threes

> *"A threefold cord is not easily broken."*
> *- The Bible, Ecclesiastes 4:12*

Agenda

The Agenda is the list of topics you will cover. For a given presentation, we recommend using three items. Why three? There are many reasons. It is easy to think in threes, and to remember three items. There is evidence that ancient man took three to be a pattern he should recognize: one is random, two is coincidence, and three establishes a pattern. The concept of thinking in threes is dominant in history and culture; for example:

- Three wishes
- Three wise men
- Three little pigs
- Three wise monkeys
- Three blind men
- Before, during and after
- Work, rest and play
- Father, Son, and Holy Ghost

- Hear no evil, see no evil, speak no evil.

So organize your individual presentations, and if possible the overall pitch, into three Agenda items.

The Body

The body is the detail of the agenda items — the data you want to convey. When using the Planner, you put in bullet points, relevant comments, and notes regarding visual aids or movement in this area.

Transitions

Transitions are connecting phrases. They serve as signposts during your talk — giving both you and the audience clear indication as to when you are moving from one section to the next. They are an important aid to your job as navigator. Transitions automatically function to heighten interest, acting as mini-grabbers. Transitions give them guidance to the map. *Don't make them think.*

Transitions can be as simple as:

- "The first agenda item is…"
- "Moving to agenda item two…"
- "Finally…"
- "In summary, the three key things to remember are…"

Transitions come in different types. They help you lead in to your content clearly, move between your Agenda topics, and set up your Close. All transitions are important for signposting your pitch, but the most important transition is the one before you close.

The Close

Avoid leaving your audience hanging or feeling like they are running off a cliff. The Close is where you leave the audience with your key takeaways and/or ask for the business. The Close includes two key elements: Summary and Closing Remarks.

Summary

The summary is what you want to leave with the audience. Use the two or three most important takeaways from your pitch. The Summary is not a restatement of the Agenda items (which are usually nouns). It's more than that. It is meant to restate the *salient points*: ensure it has enough adjectives and verbs to drive the message home. I encourage presenters to ask themselves, "If they heard only the summary, would they get the key messages?"

Next Steps and Action Items

This is where you ask for action: the next meeting, the pilot, or signature on the contract. Your Objective comes in here. What do I want them to do? Do I ask specifically here? How?

One of the biggest issues with many people in business development is their unwillingness or inability to ask for the business. You have done much to get here. You have done your homework. You have taken the time to understand the prospect and the competition. You have talked the prospect's language, told relevant stories, and demonstrated the benefits of your approach. Wrap it up strongly: let the prospect know you want to work with him. Ask for the action.

Pitch Presentation Planner

In the next few pages you will see a blank Planner, and a simple example. Use the Pitch Presentation Planner for any talk you will give to lend structure and focus the message.

Pitch Presentation Planner

Objective:

    1.

    2.

    3.

Audience:

Logistics:

Total Time:	Date of Delivery:
Time: Slide 1 (if desired)	Introduction:
	Presentation Outline
Time: Slide	Agenda 1:

Time: Slide	Agenda 2:
Time: Slide	Agenda 3:
Time:	Close
	Summary:
	Next steps:

Example Pitch Presentation Planner

Objective: [Do, Think, Feel]

    1. To motivate audience to

    2. To convince them

    3.

Audience:

Logistics: - time, audience size, room size

Total Time:	Date of Delivery:
Time: Slide 1 (if desired)	Introduction: • Grabber or Creative opening (story, shocking statistic, etc). • Subject • Why? (Authority: why listen to you?) • Objective: • Special instructions, facilities, etc
	Presentation Outline

Time:
 	
Slide
	Agenda 1: Why am I presenting this agenda item?
	First Agenda: Cultural Change
	
	• Objective
	Objective: Prove a Cultural Change is needed to win
	
	  • Anecdote or story
	
	  •
	
	  •
	
	Perhaps more here....

Time:
 	
Slide
	Agenda 2: Why am I presenting this agenda item?
	Second Agenda: Paperwork and procedures
	
	• Objective: Prove we are able to overcome obstacles (with examples as possible)
	
	     •
	
	     •
	
	     •
	
	     Transition: Getting both sides of the equation right – delivering an easier place to work by removing inefficient processes – and being obsessive about being the best and beating the competition – will take us to the front of the pack!

Time:
 	
Slide
	Agenda 3: Why am I presenting this agenda item?
	Third Agenda: Paperwork and procedures
	
	• Objective: Lay out a clear action plan to convince the audience they can change for the better. Show the benefits.
	
	     •
	
	     •
	
	     •
	
	     (Need more clarity here…)

Time:	Close
	Summary: The key takeaway points
	Next steps: ask for action [remember Objective]

Visual Aids

"I hear and I forget; I see and I remember; I do and I understand."
- Chinese proverb

Today, developing the message almost always involves creating PowerPoint slides and other materials, including possibly a pitch book. First, let's talk about the wonders of PowerPoint. Having recently celebrated its 25th birthday, PowerPoint has changed how we train, teach, and present. Today, it is estimated that there are 300 million users of PowerPoint, and over a million presentations are going on right now.

We discussed this tool before. There are many clear benefits to using PowerPoint. It helps people who use visual aids to add to their talk. As the Chinese proverb relates, it helps in memory and retention. With powerful graphics and video capability, it has become a veritable toolbox of graphic functions.

Despite the above benefits, when I ask business audiences about their perceptions of PowerPoint, I invariably get the following responses:

- Too much on the slides (words, graphics, charts)
- Can't read them (the eye test)
- A Data Dump
- Don't see the point

Picture yourself in the audience. I'm sure most of you have been there! What is the effect of most PowerPoint presentations? If you're like the majority of my clients, you answered "tune out" or "glaze over." One person said, "Blackberry time." It's just too hard to try to read and understand. Is this the effect the presenter intended? I doubt it. So what's the problem?

Different Functions

The main reason people tune out is that presenters forget that words projected on a wall during a presentation have an *entirely different function* from words printed on paper to be read. They use the same thought processes and techniques they use when preparing a document or a report. They are using the wrong tool to convey the thoughts. They create slides with heavy text and highly detailed tables, charts, and graphs — often all on the same page: a Data Dump. The audience can't read and follow it, so they don't get the point. This flood of data is guaranteed to lead to "Death by PowerPoint." We joke about it, but the very *real cost* of "Death by PowerPoint" is huge. Bad presentations lead to poor communication, which leads to poor relationships; these in turn lead to fewer sales and less revenue. A vicious circle.

The Vicious Circle of Poor Communication

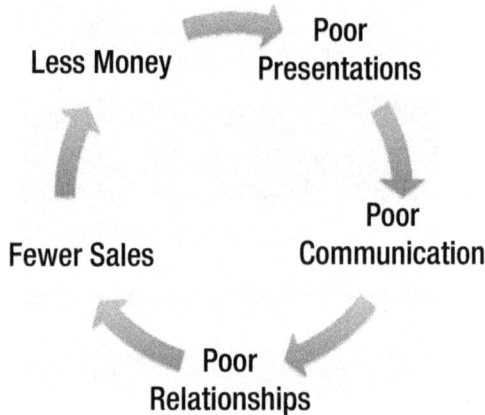

Less Money → **Poor Presentations** → **Poor Communication** → **Poor Relationships** → **Fewer Sales** →

What's more, in some organizations, the PowerPoint "document" has taken the place of the presentation. It's seen as a stand-alone document, a handout, as speaker notes. Sometimes I am told that a person "needs complex slides to show legitimacy…to show we've done our homework"! I would suggest that those who do their homework need *fewer* PowerPoints, not more.

Another example was the partner from a major business consultancy I had the dubious pleasure of working with some time ago. The team and I had carefully cast the pitch and crafted the story for weeks, rehearsed at length, and were conducting the dress rehearsal on-site.

Flying in from New York, elbowing his way into the action, the man actually called the speaker a "voice-over" for the slides! (You probably can guess we didn't exactly hit it off after that comment.) People buy from people, not slides — and not voice-overs.

The people in these examples are confused. They don't understand the use of the tool. And they are killing prospects by the millions daily. Now you know — and you can stop the carnage.

A Single Function

The key rule: a PowerPoint deck or slide set is *not* a document. A PowerPoint presentation has a *single* function: it's a pure play. It is *only* a presentation. It is a speaker and audience support. It is not the main event. It is not a document. To create a document, use a word processor. If you try to use a hammer to do the job of a screwdriver, your results suffer. Use the right tool.

If you need handouts, you can print the Notes Page view. I suggest you distribute the handouts *after* the pitch. Let them know you'll do this when you set up the pitch — in your Opening Remarks. If the prospect has them in advance, it's a sure bet they will not listen to what you are saying — they will be flipping through the deck distractedly, trying to understand slide 10 while you are on slide 2.

But what about the times when you are asked to provide a copy of the presentation for a pitch beforehand so it can be printed in a book for handouts? There are several solutions:

1. Politely offer to provide a business plan, term sheet, or executive summary — as a *document* created in Word, not PowerPoint;

2. Print some (no law says you have to do them all) slides with Notes pages; or as my team did one time,

3. Politely tell them you have *no* PowerPoints — that you will give the talk on the white board. Now that will make you stand out right away in today's PowerPoint-obsessed world!

Use the right tool for the job, and breathe *life* into your audience.

Less is More

"The ability to simplify means to eliminate the unnecessary so that the necessary may speak."

- Hans Hofmann

Minimalist architect Ludwig Mies van der Rohe adopted the motto "less is more" to describe his aesthetic tactic of arranging the numerous necessary components of a building to create an impression of extreme simplicity.[4] "Less is more" is first found in print in *Andrea del Sarto*, a poem written in 1855 by Robert Browning. Fundamentally, it means that simplicity and clarity lead to good design. "Less is more" is also a basic tenet of good presentation design, whether we are referring to the content, the length, or the slides. Less is more focused, more interesting, and more impactful.

Bullets Kill

Bullets kill people, but too many bullet points plus too much text equals information overload — "Death by PowerPoint." Typical PowerPoint presentations have 40 words per slide. There are two fundamental problems with this much text: one, we cannot take it all in — we tune out — and two, text must be interpreted by the brain before it can be understood.

The Myth of Multitasking

It's a well-documented fact that we can only concentrate on one thing at one time. Sure, you can walk and chew gum, but you cannot play complex music on the piano and solve quadratic equations simultaneously. Be skeptical when your 14-year-old son tells you he is doing his homework on a laptop with nine windows open, including two IM chats, while downloading a file, surfing Facebook, listening to his iPod, and grabbing the phone for a quick chat. This is not multitasking. It is jumping from one task to the other — task switching.

The human brain is *sequential.* It simply cannot work in parallel, or multitask. Your son's brain has to remember where it was every time your son jumps from task to task, and this takes time. In fact, studies show that a person who is interrupted takes 50 percent longer to accomplish a task. Even more disturbing, in our hectic do-it-all-now world, that person makes 50 percent more errors.

Multitasking Exercise

You are going to execute three projects, first using multitasking (task switching), and then without switching. Make three columns on a page for three projects X, Y, and Z. For the first project (column), write the numbers 1–10; in the second column write the letters A–J; and in the last column the Roman numerals I–X. You'll perform these three projects twice.

Project X	Project Y	Project Z
1	A	I
2	B	II
.	.	.
.	.	.
.	.	.
10	J	X

Start with the multitasking scenario, which involves completing one *row* at a time. Record the first character for all three sequences, then the second character for all three, and through to the tenth characters — row by row — until all three projects are completed. Be sure to time yourself.

Project X	Project Y	Project Z

10		

Now start the non-multitasking scenario, which is where you start one project, complete it, and then start the next project. In other words, you should start with *column* 1 and write down the page 1—10, then move to the second column and write A—J, then move to the next column writing I—X — column by column. Remember to time yourself.

Project X	Project Y	Project Z
10		

Now, compare your times. Also, note if you made any errors along the way. Even without the times, which one 'felt' slower or more comfortable to you?

So what does this have to do with PowerPoint pitches? When your text-heavy slide appears, and you simultaneously start talking away, your prospect cannot take it all in. He cannot multitask. Assuming he wants to understand (and doesn't tune out like some people in the audience), he must make a choice either to listen to you or to read. In either case, he misses some of your brilliant argument as to why he should work with you. This effect is compounded for those presenters and slides which have no clear point, where the written words conflict with the spoken, and where there are other distractions such as poor word choice, poorly-chosen graphics, or misspellings. It's just more corporate carnage.

Complex Little Art Museum Masterpieces

Text must be read, recognized, and interpreted by the brain to be understood. That takes effort and time. According to John Medina, the director of the Brain Center for Applied Learning Research in Seattle, "One of the reasons that text is less capable than pictures is that the brain sees words as lots of tiny pictures. Data clearly show that a word is unreadable unless the brain can separately identify simple features in the letters. Instead of words, we see complex little art museum masterpieces, with hundreds of features embedded in hundreds of letters...to our cortex, there is no such thing as words." But, you say, "I can read very, very well; we all can, so no big problem."

Medina goes on to say, "No matter how experienced a reader you become, you will still stop and ponder individual textual features as you plow through these pages, and you will continue to do so until you can't read anymore."[5] I know my Chinese clients will agree with this statement, as Mandarin consists of many more pictorial elements than English. So what should you do?

Worth a Thousand Words

The more visual the input, the more likely it is to be recognized and recalled. Pictures trump text — dramatically, and every time. In a test, people could remember 2500 pictures with at least 90 percent accuracy for several days after exposure, even though they saw each one only for 10 seconds. Accuracy rates a year later were about 63 percent. Picture recognition can last decades. (That's how my great aunt could remember all those cousins in the old family pictures so long ago).

Pictures Beat Text — Every Time

The Chinese saying is supported by the data: information presented orally has a retention rate of about 10 percent. Add a picture, and that figure goes up to about 65 percent. Minimize bullets to keep from killing your prospects. When Pitching to Win, use pictures, graphs, and graphics.

Pitch Books

Pitch books are used routinely in IPOs and for many financial pitches. They are not used in some industries at all. The main reasons for their use are to give the pitch a structure, to give details on the firm's capabilities, and to lend credibility to the products and services discussed. They often form a key leave-behind document.

If your industry uses pitch books, you probably have taken them to a pitch, thinking they would lend great support and credibility to the discussion. Did they? They may actually have detracted from the meeting. Why? Let's examine the common Pitch Book to better understand its use and abuse.

Many pitch teams will sit down with the client, and "go through" the pitch book, page by page, detail by detail, and product by product. This is a recipe for disaster. You likely are boring the prospect with an irrelevant Data Dump, talking about your products and not their problems. Often you are sitting, and your ability to control the meeting's energy is limited. We talk more later abut controlling the energy.

When pitch books fall short, it is often due to lack of customization.

Please remember, again, the client is not interested in you except for what you can do for them. As we've discussed in detail, the pitch is about the client or prospect; it's not about you or your firm. Most pitch books I've worked with are "all about us." In one recent example of a 67-page pitch book had the first 10 pages completely dedicated to the pitching firm. Not one word about the client or prospect could be found until page 11 — and that was only a generic reference.

So pitch books generally suffer from the following:

- lack of customization to the specific pitch and prospect, and
- being far too detailed in areas in which the prospect is not interested

In short, they have too much irrelevant information — which leads to "Death by Pitch Book"!

If you think about it, the two audience questions to address with a Pitch Book are:

1. What benefit would be derived for my organization and me if I use this service? and

2. Why choose this provider?

How do you create a Winning Pitch book? Answer these questions. I suggest the following:

1. If you must use a generic pitch book (generally only when you don't have an ongoing relationship), minimize focus on the *all about us* pages. The prospect likely doesn't care about your global offices, your fantastic team, and your industry awards. Go back to your Objective. Ask the WIIFM question. Then pick only the relevant pages — those that have a direct benefit to the prospect. During the meeting, ask questions to understand needs, and move to those products or services in the book quickly.

2. When you know the client, and it's a cross-sell or upsell opportunity, I suggest you don't use a generic pitch book at all. Create a simple, five-page book which gives relevant details of the deal you are pursuing or the service you are proposing. Create an Executive Summary. Then ask questions

to steer you even more specifically toward your goal, and listen.

3. Use the techniques discussed in this book to structure your talk, to better understand your prospect, and to persuade the buyer to action. This is the essence of Pitching to Win.

Summary

- Put away your normal business planning notions, and start right — by brainstorming your story, and then clustering key concepts.

- A good pitch has a clear flow so the audience can easily follow along. You are the navigator.

- *You first* is not only good manners, it's good persuasive communication.

- Well-crafted stories with a clear point engage your audience and make a memorable impression.

- Spike audience attention with Grabbers every 8 to 10 minutes (or more often).

- Help your audience navigate your pitch by using the Pitch Planner.

- Less is more.

- Bullets kill.

- Pictures trump text every time.

- Pitching to Win means using customized pitch book presentations.

Rehearse

"The secret of success in life is for a man to be ready for his opportunity when it comes."

- Benjamin Disraeli

"Winging It"

I'm often baffled and entertained by the number — and the creativity — of reasons business people can find to avoid practice and rehearsal. "We did this last month; we don't need to rehearse." Of course, we have a completely different audience and we have a couple of new people on our team. "I'm an experienced presenter." Most likely, this is a boring, read-the-slides type. And the classic, "We don't have time — we'll 'wing it', and it'll come across as fresh." More likely, you'll fumble, look unprofessional, and it will fail — right in front of the client.

It's true that most successful people in business are too busy *living* their stories to take much time to focus on *telling* their stories. While they will take some time to create a presentation, they won't take the opportunity to practice its delivery; therefore, any effort put in to this point may be wasted — an opportunity squandered.

It's simple. Professionals rehearse. They turn *unknowns* into *knowns*. Professional golfers usually arrive on the Monday and play the course a number of times before playing for money on Saturday. They hit thousands of balls in practice a week. You wouldn't expect to turn up at a professional golf tournament to find the players rushing in from airplanes and taxis, breathless as they get their gear together, and not having talked with their caddies, hit a ball, or walked the course beforehand. But that's equivalent to what I routinely see business professionals do — they arrive disorganized, uncoordinated, and without knowing the "course."

These busy people may have met their team in the taxi on the way to the client! They practice in front of the client — in front of the cameras on Saturday rather than on the driving range beforehand. They routinely shank the ball and land in the rough — not achieving the results of which they are capable because of their lack of preparation. They may be skilled, and they may have a great product, but they finish "out of the money" and they lose sales due to their unprofessional preparation.

Lincoln and the "*Four P's*"

It is worth telling the real story of Abraham Lincoln and the Gettysburg Address. Every child educated in the U.S. learned that he wrote this short speech on the back of an envelope. The implication is that he dashed off this masterful piece of writing in moments, and that he "winged it." There are a number of variations on this anecdote. This story makes business people feel comfortable with their lack of preparation and practice in their supposed emulation of the great President.

In *Lincoln at Gettysburg*, Garry Wills' Pulitzer Prize-winning book, he describes a number of variations on the myth. The speech was said to have been written on a piece of cardboard, penciling it on the night before the dedication, and even composing it in his head as the prior politician spoke.[6] The truth is far from the myth. As Garry Wills describes, the Gettysburg Address grew out of Lincoln's immersion in classical literature, the Bible, a lifetime of reading, study and practice in the law, and his admiration of oratory. Wills even tells us how Lincoln learned. "This surely is the secret of Lincoln's eloquence: he not only read aloud, to think his way into sounds, but wrote as a way of ordering his thoughts." In other words, he read it, and talked it aloud, using spaced learning over time. Wills even cites several pieces of evidence indicating that Lincoln developed the talk in Washington at least two days before the delivery, and continued to work on it during the trip to the Gettysburg site. Then, he rose "with a sheet or two" and delivered a masterpiece of prose and brevity in just 272 words.

Lincoln practiced the old saying: Proper Preparation Prevents Poor Performance. My positive version of this saying for pitching is

"Properly Prepared Pitches Prevail!" I call this the *Four P's*. As we will discuss, reading, talking, and repetitive learning, all are techniques that the properly prepared presenter will follow.

> Remember the *Four P's*: Properly Prepared Pitches Prevail!

An additional note on the Gettysburg Address: not only did Lincoln carefully prepare, his talk was a model of brevity. Nobody remembers the two-hour oratory of the previous speaker, Edward Everett, but we do have his remark to Lincoln: "I should be glad if I could flatter myself that I came as near to the central idea of the occasion in two hours, as you did in two minutes." Less is, indeed, more.

Read Through

Read Through is the process we all learned in school. It's a mental process. Once you have your script, bullet points, notes, etc., take your presentation and read it through, paragraph by paragraph. Hone it and polish. Clarify. Look for cumbersome words and sentences. Don't use a $10 word when a $5 word will do. Think of the audience. Do they have your language as their second language? Will they understand this?

The Sharpening Stone

As you do this, get more focus: think as if you were the decision maker in the audience. *Hone your content* against the sharpening stone of your audience understanding and your objective. Make it sharper and sharper, like an knife on a sharpening stone. At the end of each paragraph, stop and ask yourself: Would I (as the decision maker) understand that? Do I care? So what? Does this statement help to meet the objective? What does that mean to me, as a prospect? By being *ruthlessly* critical and thinking like the prospective audience, you will be able to cut unwanted material and to sharpen the message.

Talk Through

This is the first step in physical rehearsal. In this step, you actually speak the presentation out loud. This is the only way you'll really crystallize the ideas in your mind. Many business people bridle at this step when I'm coaching them, saying, "I'll just talk you through it." You can no more learn your presentation by talking about it than you can improve your swing by talking about golf. Actually deliver it. The more you speak the pitch out loud, the more comfort you will have when presenting. I suggest you do it several times for new material. Even better, speak it into a recorder, and listen to yourself. Do you sound confident, professional, and interesting? Go ahead. You can do it.

When you do this, you will again find cumbersome sentences and words. We tend to write at a higher level of language and precision than we speak. We use larger words and sentences. Now is when you personalize your pitch, making it sound the way you talk; making it warmer and less stilted. Make it yours. Continue to hone it against the objective and audience. Continue to ask, "Will they care?" You will find that you can make your points clearer and clearer as you trim and focus. Each time you rehearse, you will find something that could be better.

How Do You Learn?

I am often asked the best way to get from the printed page (script, bullet points, slides, etc.) to the brain. There is no one answer to this question. Different people learn differently. I have worked with people who could never memorize or readily verbalize the talk successfully without notes to those who looked it over once, and soaked it up (what a nice skill to have!). One thing I do know: distributed learning over time, works best.[7] Distributed learning is the opposite of "cramming." Space your practice out over time. Rehearse, rehearse, take a break — a few hours or days — and then rehearse some more.

The Pitch Team

Team presentations are similar to individual presentations in that both rely on the same fundamentals — understanding the audience, setting objectives, preparing, structuring, and then delivering the presentation with the right skills and techniques.

But the similarities pretty much end there, and the recognition that you're now part of a team becomes all-important. A Winning Pitch team presentation will come off as just that: a *team* presentation.

The team leader's job is to facilitate the process of deciding objectives and key messages. It is critical for the team members to buy into the team's goals and key messages. They should understand and accept that they will work as and succeed only as a team, with clear goals. I suggest focusing on the three essential goals you as a team want to achieve from the pitch. Individually, you can build subsets of these overall goals, with everything aligned to those priorities that the team together has agreed upon.

Next, decide upon an overarching theme that ties the individual presentations together. Be careful of using trite themes such as "Your Long-Term Business Partner." These have been so misused over the years; you're better off keeping it subtle. You can then begin to see the unifying elements within the overall scheme and how they link to one another.

"Chance favors the prepared mind."

–Louis Pasteur

Team Preparation Is Critical (The *Four P's* Squared)

Preparation is even more essential to a team than it is to a solo presentation. I often say these presentations have "more moving parts," and usually much more information to share; therefore, they have more things to go wrong, to clarify, and to get ironed out before the pitch.

As you prepare, organize your individual presentations as if they were each part of one continuous presentation which will be spoken by several people. Strive for consistency in delivery, "look and feel," and work together to create a cohesive whole; not a bunch of disjointed monologues. It may help to think of these as chapters in a book, with a story line running through the book leading to a specific end.

Preparation Checklist
• How much time does each presenter have?
• How much time for the total presentation?
• In what order will everyone present?
• Will there be questions during your presentation or afterwards?
• Who will precede you and who will follow you?
• How can you link your remarks to theirs?
• Will the meeting have a moderator? If not, who will introduce you?
• What kind of introduction will you have?
• How can your introduction be made to help set up your remarks?
• Will you introduce the next presenter? At what length? (Consistency counts here!)
• How is the room set up?
• Will you be seated, will you be at a podium, or will you be simply standing?
• What is the audience size?
• What equipment will you be using?
• Will others be joining your meeting via phone or video?

Transitions are key to making the team pitch flow properly. Just as in an individual presentation, transitions are elements that signpost the road map and help navigate the pitch. Each presenter will wrap up his or her own segment, and then establish a link to the next presenter. It's useful, when appropriate, for each presenter to include brief references to the key points made by the other speakers. This reinforces the team cohesiveness and the key messages, and helps your audience retain information.

It is critical to stick to your time limit. If you have been involved in a "beauty pageant" where you had a strict time limit and were shown the door exactly at the conclusion of that time, you can relate. If a couple of presenters run long and you are unable to conclude, summarize, and ask for the business, it results in a huge waste of time and resources, and a major lost opportunity. When you plan, cut your allocated time by 10 or 15 percent. I rehearse every team to finish a few minutes early. Then, you don't feel the need to rush as there is no danger of running long, and you have extra time for Q&A if needed. If you do make your points well and finish early, it will be like a breath of fresh air for everyone. Nobody will complain if you are a few minutes short!

The best practice is to appoint a person to be the "traffic cop" for Q&A. Often, this will be the senior member of the pitch team. During the Q&A period, beware the extremes of either dominating the responses or taking no questions. Be quick to redirect a question to others if it is related more to their area of expertise than to yours. Be ready also to add to someone else's response if it relates in some way to your topic. How your team manages Q&A is critical to the client seeing you as a team: how you deal with tough questions here can indicate to him how you will handle problems if he hires you for the job.

Below are a few tips for team pitching, both during the delivery and while handling Q&A:

- Make sure everyone understands his or her role.

- Once you've finished speaking, introduce the next speaker as appropriate. Then clear your space and move away.

- Use a consistent style of visual aids for all speakers to create a unified appearance.

- The person speaking is in charge; don't interrupt unless absolutely necessary.

- Stay on script — you have taken the time to plan, share, and rehearse the presentation together; allow no last minute changes without a compelling reason, and without discussing it with the team.

- Critical: stick to your time limit. If you have ten minutes, I suggest you rehearse to eight.

Walk Through

After Talk Through, do a Walk Through. This second step in physical rehearsal consists of standing and delivering the pitch. You can do this wherever you are, but it's best if you can do it in a room similar to (ideally the same room) the one in which you will present.

For this to be most effective, have some audience members in attendance and use a video camera. Family members who care for you are great for this. People at the office also can be "volunteered." I once worked with an executive who prevailed upon his wife and his 14-year-old son to the point where he said they knew the pitch as well as he did! And yes, you can video yourself. The camera doesn't lie. Cameras are inexpensive and readily available today. It is very useful to see how you come across on video.

Why use video in rehearsal?

I once had a senior-level corporate executive client who had the habit of sticking his hands in his pockets and fidgeting "down there" during his talk. He was completely unaware of it, and his staff wouldn't tell him. The unwanted job fell to me as coach. I decided to use video to do the job. We simply observed a few minutes of a presentation. He made a comment and I concurred. It was never a problem again.

Rehearse to yourself in the office (door closed if you must), in the shower, in front of a mirror, in the car, in an empty boardroom, in front of your colleagues, and in the actual presentation room you will be using. Ideally, if possible, you should do a full rehearsal in the room where you will present, with a coach and with video. But any rehearsal is better than none!

For a big pitch, you will want to do full dress rehearsal as the final Walk Through. As we know from theatre, this is a full rehearsal on the final stage, wherein the full performance is run as it will be on the opening night. We run a dress rehearsal with full lighting, slides, videos, etc., so the pitch team has a very good level of comfort with each of their parts and the overall flow, impact, and delivery. The presentation is recorded. A dress rehearsal often is where you iron out the "bugs" regarding logistics, microphones, technical issues, etc. All team pitches will be better after a dress rehearsal. If you are unable to use the actual venue, replicate it as best you can.

Summary

- Professionals rehearse.

- Practice and rehearse in advance, not in front of the prospect.

- Hone your content against the sharpening stone of your objective and audience understanding.

- Four steps of rehearsal:

    1. Read Through (a mental process)

    2. Talk Through (a physical process)

    3. Walk Through (stand and deliver)

    4. Dress Rehearsal (on location, with props)

Deliver the Story

The Pitch

"The problem with communication is the illusion that it has occurred."
- George Bernard Shaw

The Beauty Pageant

An audience of seven executives shuffles into their seats as a team of three enters the room and prepares to present. The afternoon is getting long. The hotel buffet lunch is languishing in the audience members' stomachs, while the coffee has turned bitter. This is the third pitch of the day, with another yet to endure. All the pitches cover similar ground in response to the RFP instructions. All the presenters promise great products and superior customer service. On and on it goes, while the audience struggles to make out differences between the offers, and sometimes even to stay awake.

Sound familiar? This is the problem the pitch team often faces. Even when there are fewer presentations, or they are spread out over more time, the prospect's team will see similar presentations, hear similar promises, and have similar discussions.

For many years in my career, I didn't believe this. I thought our company was so far superior; we were the clear first choice. Then one day, one of my coaches in a large account let my competitor's pitch document "fall" into my briefcase. When I got back to the office, we looked at it in detail. What an eye opener! The colors and logos were different, but the logic, the general argument, and even some of the graphics were virtually identical to ours! It was almost as if we had consulted together; and that was definitely not the case. So don't be misled. Your offer will be similar in many respects to the competitors'. What to do?

The good news is that if you have done your background digging, your hard work and preparation can now pay off. You have the *critical edge* — an understanding of the prospect's need to buy, the organization, and the process. You speak to the buyer's needs in their language, offering relevant benefits, and your team is well-positioned to come out on top. The critical edge is just that — an edge. You don't have to be far, far superior.

At the top levels, the differences become smaller and smaller. But the benefits to the winner become larger and larger. For example, Tiger Woods, clearly the top professional golfer in 2008, shot about four percent better than the second tier of golfers. That's only a couple of strokes a round. Not really much. However, Tiger's winnings in 2008 were more than *ten times* those of the second tier. As my manager used to say, "The lead sled dog isn't far ahead, but he has a much better view!"

First Impressions

> *"There is no truth. There is only perception."*
>
> *- Gustave Flaubert*

According to Malcolm Gladwell, in the book *Blink*, "When you meet someone for the first time, or walk into a house you are thinking of buying, or read the first few sentences of a book, your mind takes about two seconds to jump to a series of conclusions." We all create and respond to first impressions. The old adage that you never get a second chance to make a first impression is true. Right or wrong, first impressions count! How do we ensure our first impressions are positive and professional?

Right now, before you have to prepare for a meeting or a pitch, take a hard, objective look at yourself. Consider how you enter a room. Consider your image. This includes the following:

- Posture and body language
- Voice
- Eye contact
- Breathing
- Breath

- Scent
- Clothing
- Confidence

Consider also your handshake, your focus, your conversation, your concentration, preparation, intention, timing, and use of humor. Do these convey the positive images you want to project? Or are you slumping, distracted, nervous, and fidgety? Your first impression is in your control. Make it the one you want!

"We are evaluated and classified by these four contacts: what we do, how we look, what we say, and how we say it."

- Dale Carnegie

Here is a simple trick that can help. Walk into a room like you are walking in to meet the President at a gala reception. Hold a strong, upright posture. Give a strong, firm handshake and make eye contact with a warm, sincere smile. Sure, you may be nervous. But your preparation, concentration, and intention will broadcast to all that you are poised and professional.

Introductions

"Effective communication is 20 percent what you know and 80 percent how you feel about what you know."

- Jim Rohn

The big day finally has arrived. Your team has burned the midnight oil to understand the opportunity and create a Winning Pitch. Everyone has rehearsed until a mutiny is imminent. Now, how do you manage the introductions while you are remembering all the background details — thinking of what you need to say, sizing up the situation, and hoping you handle the business card appropriately?

The key is to focus on the other person. Drop competing thoughts, just for a moment. When you are distracted, your body language will give you away. Do this by practicing a simple mental trick. Pretend the other person is an old friend or customer for whom you have great admiration, and who's been out of your life for a long time. Suddenly, there they are! How glad you are to see them, and how grateful they have shown up today! Your facial and body expressions will change — you will light up when introducing yourself. Just do this for a moment, and that's all it takes for the other to feel very special.

Introducing Your Team

I'm often asked how to introduce the team. Should everyone be introduced at the beginning, or should this be done as they rise to speak? Should they do it themselves, or should a moderator intervene? It's not as simple a question as it first appears. The answer depends upon the situation, and varies according to the audience, setting, culture, and formality of the customer.

Experience has shown it's good to have something of a mix of introductions. I suggest that the team leader (or possibly senior manager) introduce everyone, giving job titles and roles, as a part of the opening remarks. Then, when a given speaker takes the stage, she can relate a couple of sentences with more introduction — possibly talking about her years of experience in this line of work. This hybrid approach serves multiple purposes. First, the audience knows who everyone is at the beginning, without having to guess. Second, the process itself demonstrates leadership control with teamwork. Also, and importantly, each speaker gets a chance to build credibility while talking about themselves. And that's a good way to start your portion of the pitch.

What about taking along people who won't pitch? It surprises me how often teams want to take along others, whether they have been involved in the business up to now or not. Sometimes many people want to be involved — too many. We once called this "filling the bus." Refer back to the discussion on staffing your team. Ask a simple question, "What is their role?" If their role is to *show management interest*, or be there *just in case*, I would suggest they stay behind. Everyone who goes to the pitch event should have a clear purpose for being there. Usually, they all should present. Even if they come along only for Q&A, include them by introducing them in the beginning. In summary, in the Winning Pitch, everyone has a role. They are clearly aware of that role, and they stick to it.

Just Before You Speak: Handling Nerves

You're about to make a presentation when suddenly you realize your stomach is doing cartwheels, your palms are sweaty — and is that perspiration running down from your armpits? Not only that, but you sense your mind is rapidly going blank.

"How do I handle this critical time period?" "How do I deal with the 'jitters'?" People ask me these questions often in my coaching sessions and classes. There is no single answer for every situation. The simple answer is *prepare*. Take unknowns and turn them into knowns by preparing mentally and physically.

Physical Preparation

When Pitching to Win, spend much more time preparing than you will spend speaking. Depending on the situation, the audience, and your objectives, people who want to win will spend ten to twenty times as much time in preparation as they do actually presenting. Sometimes this preparation time is less, but all preparation will help you overcome the nerves. Remember the *Four P's*: Properly prepared pitches prevail.

People will decide whether you are credible very quickly — within the first minute. And we know the interest is usually high in the beginning. Therefore, it's critical to get the opening right. *Nail the opening!* But this is generally the most difficult part of a presentation — and it's often where people fumble. I wonder how many times I've heard, "Good morning…ahhh…" If you struggle with this, a great way to start well is to memorize your opening and closing — just three or four sentences of each. Then you can refer to notes if needed. Memorizing your opening and closing lets you start credibly and end fluently, allowing you to connect with your audience during these critical moments.

Professionals turn unknowns into knowns. Visit the venue well before your talk. Walk around the room; get a feel for the acoustics, the lighting, the "energy," and any possible distractions (such as a loud air conditioner, windows to outside, etc.). Get comfortable in the environment. If you will be speaking from a stage, go early and walk the stage. Try out your voice and "feel" the environment. Then, during your presentation, you can concentrate on your audience, and not your environment.

Avoid "Deer in the Headlights Syndrome"

I worked with a senior executive who ran a very successful business, but who was having great difficulty speaking with the impact and command that his job required. The first time we met, he admitted to me that he had just spoken to 600 people without ever seeing the room. When we watched the video, he looked for the first minute like a "deer in the headlights." A person experiencing "deer in headlights syndrome" often shows behavioral signs reminding one of a deer in the darkness suddenly subjected to a car's headlights: widely opened eyes, anxiety, fear, and confusion. He didn't connect at all with the audience, as he was taking in all aspects of the room in the first few seconds; figuring out the microphone, the podium, etc. He started poorly, and was off-track from the beginning. That was no way to start. After we saw the video and discussed the result, he vowed never to go cold into a presentation room again.

If possible, before you speak, I suggest you go around the group shaking hands and making eye contact with everybody. For larger meetings, meet and shake hands with whomever you can — people at the coffee bar, people coming in the front door, etc. Most people want you to succeed. When you connect with them personally, they'll be even more likely to support your success. This is another way to turn unknowns into knowns. Speakers are rarely nervous about individuals; only the mass called "an audience." Once you've met the audience, or at least some of them, they become much less intimidating.

It's totally natural to be nervous. You may want to try this acting technique. Find a private spot, and wave your hands in the air. Relax and massage your jaw — a place where tension accumulates — then shake your head from side to side. Then shake your legs one at a time. Physically *shake* the tension out of your body. (Comedian Robin Williams is known for doing "jumping jacks" before going on stage to reduce tension and raise his energy level.)

Now *breathe*. Really breathe with your diaphragm. This is how babies breathe. Place one hand on your upper chest and one on your stomach. Take a breath and let your stomach swell like a balloon as you breathe in, and compress it back towards your spine as you breathe out. To get a steady rhythm going, take the same depth of long breath each time. Your hand on your chest should have little movement. When you feel comfortable with this technique, slow your breathing rate down by allowing a short pause after you have breathed out and before you breathe in again. Initially, it may feel as though you are not getting enough air in, but with regular practice this slower rate will soon start to feel comfortable.

Try not to sit down too much while you're waiting to speak. If you're scheduled to go on an hour into the program, sit in the back of the room if you can, so that you can stand up occasionally. It is hard to jump up and be dynamic when you've been relaxed in a chair for hour. Sitting in the back also gives you easy access to the facilities and drinking fountain. There's nothing worse than being stuck down front and being distracted by urgent bodily sensations.

Mental Preparation

Mental preparation is every bit as valuable as physical preparation.

Visualize

The subconscious brain cannot tell the difference between scenes that are vividly imagined and those that actually occur. Professionals in all walks of life use visualization to improve performance. Professional golf great Jack Nicklaus once said he practiced the course dozens of times, before arriving — he played the course over and over again in his mind. He visualized hitting shots long and straight, and landing on the greens just as planned. When the actual event came, he was mentally ready. Professional entertainers and athletes go over their acts and their lines mentally countless times — visualizing the scene, seeing themselves making each move perfectly, and watching the positive response from the audience.

Unfortunately, many business professionals do not use the power of visualization. Or, if they do, they use it negatively — thinking of what could go wrong, sweating that they are not up to the task, or otherwise tearing themselves down. Jack Nicklaus never said "I think I'll shank the ball." But many speakers effectively do the same thing, telling themselves, "I'm just not a good presenter." No, Nicklaus would have visualized the positive and said, "I'm going to hit it solid, give it a ride about 280 yards, and set myself up to win." You can do something similar when you visualize success.

Affirm

When I coach advanced presenters, I work with them to create an affirmation — a simple, positive aspirational statement based on fact — that they can repeat to themselves just before speaking. Every one is different. Each person should believe it. An example might be, "When I make good eye contact and smile, I am a confident, persuasive presenter." Another one is, "I'm going to nail the opening and close." Visualize a successful pitch.

Finally, remember those "jitters" are your friend. They sharpen your reflexes and get your energy level up. One of my students was a swimmer in university and related this story. When a competitive swimmer is on the blocks, his pulse is racing — major jitters. And that's good. When that swimmer hits the water, he's immediately into the flow of the race. No need to "ramp up." In fact, if he had to, he would be behind the others who had the case of nerves! So use the nerves to help you. Direct that energy into your talk and into the audience, and you will be a more dynamic, engaging speaker!

Eye Contact

"I feel that in-person contact with people is the most important thing in comedy. While I'm up on stage, I can actually put myself into the audience and adjust my pace and tuning to them. I can get into their heads through their ears and through their eyes. Only through this total communication can I really achieve what I'm trying to do."

- Bill Cosby, American actor and comedian

Have you been in a meeting where the presenter was looking at the floor, the ceiling, or out the window — but not at you? How did that make you feel?

We connect to people through our eyes. The eyes truly are the windows to the soul. I read once that the eyes are the only part of the brain that is exposed. So don't handicap yourself. Look at people in the audience. Look directly at one person as you communicate a thought — use five or six seconds of gaze time per person.

Before you speak the next sentence or thought, make eye contact with one person and hold that eye contact until you have completed the sentence or that thought. One thought per person, for five or six seconds. Then, move to another person and repeat randomly around the room. The technique itself is natural — it's how we speak to people at the dinner table or the club — but when standing and speaking, it requires practice. At first, you may find it uncomfortable. Most of us scan the audience, never really making eye contact with any one person for longer than a second or two. We don't really connect. Force yourself to linger — break the eye contact only after you have delivered a complete thought. Practice this at home; you will be pleased with the results.

Eye contact is a key factor in establishing trust. Michael Argyle, a pioneer of social psychology and nonverbal communication skills, found that when one person likes another a lot, he will look at him a lot — more than 60 percent of the time. This, in turn, causes the first person to increase eye contact, as liking increases. We call this *the build*. It's like trust — it takes time. The nervous, timid person who looks at you less than a third of the time is rarely trusted.

Clearly, there are differences in cultures. Most Asians don't connect with the eyes as strongly as do Westerners. However, the differences are not as great as the uninitiated might expect. One reason is that international business today is primarily driven by Western cultural norms. But be aware to be safe. The best rule in places such as Japan is to mirror the gaze time of your hosts. Then, you will build: you will likely notice that gaze time will build over time as comfort, intimacy, and trust grow (or may decrease if the converse occurs!).

> **Eye contact rule #1: Look at people. Don't look at computers, PowerPoint slides, or out the window. Look at people.**

A few more rules of good eye contact:

2. Don't linger too long, or stare.

3. Don't ignore anyone (be sure to *share the love*!). If someone is looking down, come back later.

4. The decision maker gets more eye contact. (But see rule 3.)

5. When presenting, connect randomly with the group. Don't be predictable (we call this effect "The Terminator").

Voice

The first rule of the voice is to be heard. But there is much more to using your voice. In my experience, the biggest problem with the voice is the tendency to speak in a monotone. Mono means one: mono + tone = one tone = *boring*. Whether you are very loud, very fast, or very soft, if you continue for 20 minutes in that same vein, your audience will tune you out.

So to increase engagement, use variety. Vary your tone, your pace, your volume, and even your projection. Think of an excited child. Think of an impassioned leader. They are dynamic; they vary the voice delivery. They exhibit their passion, interest, or concern with the voice. For examples of this, check out your favorite character actor's latest movie. Listen to quality radio broadcasts or professional podcasts. How can you move beyond monotone? When you rehearse, practice adding emotion, enthusiasm, and interest. Listen to yourself. If your words and voice are convincing and engaging, you will hear it on the audio recording.

> **A recipe to improve the voice: Mix conviction with desire, and then add a good measure of rehearsal.**

Gap Fillers

Linguistics experts refer to *ums* and *ahs* as "voiced pauses." These are gap fillers — breaks between words we fill with sounds. They don't mean anything. Examples of filler words are *um, uh, ah, okay, so, you know, well, but, like*, etc. When overused, they tend to chip away at your credibility and can make you sound unsure and unprepared. The first step to reducing them is to be aware of how often you use them. I have worked with people who use *um* twenty times or more in a minute. When asked, they are completely unaware. To build awareness, use an audio or video recorder. Then ask yourself how you are coming across.

Gap fillers come about because silence is not generally acceptable in regular conversations, or you can lose your turn. We all use these noises in conversations to show we heard the other and are starting to speak, or, in the middle of our discussion, to show that we are continuing and not yet finished. For example, we might say, "um, I think that's a good idea, and...ah...let's discuss the timing..." These voiced pauses fill a need in conversations — a need to show the other we are engaged and thinking, and that we have more to say; that is, as long as they are not overused.

The reason these voiced pauses or gap fillers are so annoying in public speaking is that the problems they solve in conversations simply don't exist when presenting to a larger group. There is no need to indicate with such noises we have begun to speak, and we don't need to worry about filling silence in presentations. Nobody is likely to hijack the presentation during a speaker's pause. In fact, the opposite is the case. Skilled presenters use *pause* to allow the audience time — to digest the words spoken.

Pausing

As skilled conversationalists, we avoid the pause. As skilled presenters, we embrace the pause. Skillful use of the pause allows the audience time to contemplate and to react, and allows much more engagement than the usual monotone of one-way sentences, unremarkable one from the other. Pausing allows us to change the meaning and the mood and to readily modify our pace, keeping the presentation lively and dynamic. A pause gives the audience time to digest what's been said. In addition, a pause allows the speaker time — time to judge the audience's reaction, to look down at notes, and to think through the next topic. Embrace the pause.

Weak Words

And, while we're discussing voice...

Please be careful about your wording. Even with CEOs, I hear, "I think we are good at..." Come on — you are the CEO! Tell them. Be clear and direct. Either we are good at it or we are not. Don't water it down. You don't *think* it. You *know* it (or you don't — which message are you conveying?).

"Do or do not. There is no try."
　　　　　- *Yoda; Star Wars: Episode IV, The Empire Strikes Back (1980)*

Another pet peeve of mine is the word *try*. It's an interesting word, *try*. Its original meaning, "to make an effort," has been distorted to soften our delivery — or is it to point out our *lack* of delivery? If I say, "Try to pick up that chair," I mean, "Make an effort to pick it up." You may try and you may actually pick it up. That's very well. But you don't "try to deliver by Thursday." You deliver by Thursday or you don't. I strongly recommend you drop this word completely in your pitch. How do you feel when a supplier tells you they will *try* to deliver? I cringe. (You can imagine how much my children like my position on this one — they bought me a t-shirt with the Yoda quote.)

Another interesting word is *but*. This one (and its cousins *however* and *although*) actually negate everything that went before. Those words exclude. When your colleague says, "Tim, that's an interesting idea, but…" you can be sure she doesn't really think it's all that interesting. Instead, use the inclusive word *and*. How different it feels when she says, "Tim, that's an interesting idea, and…" Big difference. When answering a question or objection, be careful to use *and*.

Also, be careful about pronunciation. If you don't know how to pronounce a word, don't use it, or look it up in an on-line dictionary which includes the audio. Pronunciation errors are perceived as an indication of poor preparation and ignorance. You may well be put in a box by the listener — the uneducated box. Right or wrong, a person's perceptions are that person's reality.

Stay out of the box. Don't water down your message. Here's how. Unless you have a very good reason, it's best to avoid the following:

- Kinda
- Sorta
- Uh-huh
- Yeah
- I think
- Hopefully
- Try
- Basically
- Actually
- Ok (and ok and ok and ok)
- But (and however and although)
- Allows

Gestures

"Every gesture is a gesture from the blood, every expression a symbolic utterance... Everything is of the blood, of the senses."

- Henry Williamson

You've probably heard about the woman who couldn't talk if you cut off her hands. Hand gestures are natural. The human hand has more nerve connections to the brain than to other parts of the body. Perhaps this is why the gestures we make with our hands give powerful signals to our audiences. Hand gestures grab attention, add emphasis, and increase the impact of our pitch.

> **Gestures also aid recall. In a study conducted at the University of Manchester in England, volunteers listened to stories of well-known cartoon characters. For some listeners, a narrator added hand gestures such as waving the hands up and down to show movement and holding the arms far apart to indicate a fat person. When the subjects were tested 10 minutes later, those who had seen the gestures had as much as a one-third better recall of story details.**

Many people are unaware of this, but we all are hardwired to subconsciously read gestures with our primitive brain. Gestures are a universal language. Gestures can add immeasurably to a pitch.

But — just like a monotone voice — monotonous, repetitive gestures are boring. Like the voice, you can incorporate a dynamic range of gestures. The other extreme is just as bad — too many and too fast. Also, the audience will immediately read overblown or fake gestures as disingenuous. Work for *congruence*: make the words, voice, and actions say the same thing. Work for unrepetitive gestures that are relevant to the audience and the subject; they should be smooth, deliberate, and polished.

Movement

Movement is the "big brother" of gestures. Movement adds dynamism, interest, and energy to the pitch. The biggest challenge I see with movement is the "caged lion" effect. If you've ever been to the circus or a zoo with small cages, you will get the point. Repetitive, back-and-forth, rocking and swaying. Talking while randomly walking. Clearly energetic, but without a specific purpose. To be more effective, plan your movement with a purpose. When you want to make a selling point, move towards the decision maker. When dissuading, you may move subtly away. This is another area where video recording will help you improve. Watch yourself and ensure the movement and gestures are adding to the talk and not detracting from it.

Winning Presenters use the Three P's to *move with a purpose*:

Plan: Plan your movement. Choreograph your pitch.

Plant: Stop moving. Plant your feet like a football player awaiting a play.

Present: Make eye contact and speak your piece for that portion of the pitch, that audience member, etc.

As long as you are comfortable, don't be afraid to use the full front of the room or the stage. I often advise speakers to move from one side of the stage to the other. Do it at planned points in your pitch. It changes the energy and focus in the room. You can use this moment as a short break with a natural pause, giving you poise and a grounded delivery.

Then move on, and do it again. You will find you are better able to connect with the audience; and you come across as more grounded, strong, and in control — all good things.

Handling the Q&A

Listening

"The greatest compliment that was ever paid me was when one asked me what I thought, and attended to my answer."

- Henry David Thoreau

I love the symbolism in Eastern languages and traditions. Study the traditional Mandarin Chinese symbol for listening.

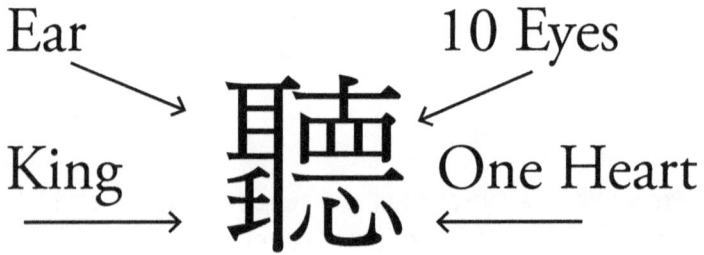

Ear   10 Eyes

聽

King   One Heart

It's clear: the ear is King; and to listen, you need ten eyes combined with one heart. You listen with ears, eyes, and heart. The questioner encodes the question in words, body language, and tone. The good listener then decodes the full meaning — using all senses.

> *Effective communication* exists between two people when the receiver interprets and understands the sender's message in the same way the sender intended it.

Barriers to Listening

Below is a list of those things that get in the way of listening. Sometimes, it's a wonder we get the message across at all!

Physical Barriers

- Background noise and competing conversations
- Visual distractions
- Hunger (thirst, other physical distractions)
- Hearing impediments (sinus, respiratory, auditory impairments)

Mental and Emotional Barriers

- Not "present" — mind elsewhere, wandering, tuned out
- Not "open" — already decided
- Disinterested, bored
- Stress, anger, dislike of speaker
- Prejudices

The more you are aware of these barriers, the more you can do to overcome them.

Three Basic Listening Modes

How often do we listen — really *listen* — to another? I suggest it's not common at home or in business. Listening consists of three general modes in a continuum.

- **Competitive or Combative Listening** happens when we are more interested in promoting our own point of view than in understanding or exploring someone else's view. We either listen for openings to take the floor, or for flaws or weak points we can attack. As we pretend to pay attention, we are either impatiently waiting for an opening or internally formulating our rebuttal and planning our devastating comeback that will destroy their argument and make us the victor.

- In **Passive or Attentive Listening**, we are genuinely interested in hearing and understanding the other person's point of view.

We are attentive and do listen. We assume that we heard and understand correctly, but stay passive and do not verify it.

- **Active or Reflective Listening** is the single most useful and important listening skill. In active listening, we also are genuinely interested in understanding what the other person is thinking, feeling, and wanting; we are active in checking out our understanding before we respond with our own new message. We restate or paraphrase our understanding of the sender's message and reflect it back to the sender for verification. This verification or reflective process is what distinguishes active listening and makes it effective.

Reflective listening is another way of rephrasing what the other person has said in a nonjudgmental manner, and then saying it back to them to make certain you have understood what they have said — not just the words, but the feelings and meanings. Reflective listening may be the most important and often underutilized skill involved in effective communication.

One of the biggest barriers to reflective listening is the notion that repeating back the ideas and feelings of the other person is to accept and agree with them. This is not the case — you are simply demonstrating that you understand what is being expressed (and you are affirming the person for expressing the thought and feeling).

This technique gives the other person the chance to correct or modify the thought or comment. It also makes them feel good because they see you making the effort to really understand what they are about. Once you have a clear understanding of what the other person has said, then you can begin to evaluate where to go from there. As Stephen Covey said, "Seek first to understand, then to be understood."

Reflection is possibly the most powerful device in our personal toolbox for relating to and working with other people. It is also very underused by most people. It is a fundamental approach toward affirmation and shared understanding.

The technique is straightforward.

- First, you listen with aggressive attention. Listen to learn. Listen without judgment. Don't assume this is easy; it requires concentration and mental discipline!

- You support this physically: lean slightly forward while you listen, maintaining good eye contact with the speaker, being calm and not fidgeting while they are talking. Give verbal feedback as they speak ("yes," "I see," "uh-huh," etc.).

- The next step is to empathize with the feelings involved. Take a few seconds to quickly remember a time when you experienced the same or a similar feeling (it doesn't have to be the same situation). The feeling is the thing that counts.

- Then you find the words that feed back the essence of what the other person is saying and feeling. Do not interpret any element of their statement. Don't guess at their motivations, for example. Just rephrase what they have told you. The interpretation comes later. You can use empathic statements such as "so you feel that..." or "I can sense that you..." to help capture the emotional qualities of what they said or how they said it.

- Feel free to *name* the feeling or emotion expressed. This is key to affirmation of the other. "So you are upset about the new policy." I call this "naming the emotion, without becoming emotional." Maintain your disciplined, cool demeanor.

- Once you have done this, then you can add your own thoughts and feelings to the situation — but only after you have fed back the critical portion. If you are off a little in your understanding, the other person will correct you. Now, you have real communication and understanding. If you were right on, they will realize that they have been understood. Rapport will skyrocket as a result.

"Listening, not imitation, may be the sincerest form of flattery."
- Dr Joyce Brothers

Benefits of Active Listening

There is a real distinction between merely hearing the words and really listening for the message. When we listen effectively, we understand what the person is thinking and feeling from the other person's perspective. It is as if we were standing in the other person's shoes, seeing through her eyes and listening through her ears. This is empathy. Our own viewpoint may be different and we may not necessarily agree with the person, but as we listen, we understand from the other's perspective.

We all act and respond on the basis of our understanding, and too often there is a misunderstanding that neither of us is aware of. With active listening, if a misunderstanding has occurred, it will be known immediately, and the communication can be clarified before any further misunderstanding occurs.

Several other possible benefits occur with active listening:

- Sometimes a person just needs to be heard and acknowledged before she is willing to consider an alternative or soften her position.

- It is usually easier for a person to listen to and consider the other's position when he knows that the other is listening and considering his position.

- It helps people to spot their reasoning flaws when they hear their words played back without criticism.

- It also helps identify areas of agreement so the areas of disagreement are put in perspective and are diminished rather than magnified.

- Reflecting back what we hear helps to give each person a chance to become aware of which of the four levels the other is operating from. Then, differences can be more readily resolved.

- If we accurately understand the other person's view, we can be more effective in helping that person see other points of view.

- If we listen so we can accurately understand the other's view, we can also be more effective in discovering the flaws in our own position.

Listening Tips

Usually it is important to paraphrase and use your own words in verbalizing your understanding of the message. Parroting back the words verbatim is annoying and does not ensure accurate understanding of the message.

Depending on the purpose of the interaction and your understanding of what is relevant, you could reflect back the other person's:

- Account of the facts

- Thoughts and beliefs

- Feelings and emotions

- Wants, needs, or motivation

- Hopes and expectations

More Tips for Improving Communication

- Don't respond to just the meaning of the words; look for the feelings or intent beyond the words. The dictionary or surface meaning of the words or code used by the sender not be the message.

- Inhibit your impulse to immediately answer questions. The code may be in the form of a question. Sometimes people ask questions when they really want to express themselves and are not open to hearing an answer.

- Know when to quit using active listening. Once you accurately understand the sender's message, it may be appropriate to respond with your own message.

- If you are confused and know you do not understand, either tell the person you don't understand and ask him to say it another way, or use your best guess. If you are incorrect, the person will realize it and will likely attempt to correct your misunderstanding.

- Use eye contact and listening body language. Avoid looking at your watch or at other people or activities around the room.

Face the speaker and lean toward him, nodding your head when appropriate. Be careful about crossing your arms and appearing closed or critical.

- Be empathic and nonjudgmental. You can be accepting and respectful of the person and their feelings and beliefs without invalidating or giving up your own position, or without agreeing with the accuracy and validity of their view.

- Become a more effective listener. Practice the active listening technique and make it one of your communication skills.

Questioning

"I keep six honest serving-men
(They taught me all I knew);
Their names are What and Why and When
And How and Where and Who."

- Rudyard Kipling

"To be able to ask a question clearly
is two-thirds of the way to getting it answered."

- John Ruskin

Sound questions based on preparation and insightful thinking project a favorable image of competence and professionalism. Preparation of good questions is critical to understanding needs. Use the techniques below both during the Prologue stage and during the Q&A stage of the pitch, as you work to better understand the prospect's needs.

Purposes of probing include:

- to obtain information (turn unknowns into knowns)
- to open discussion
- to help the other person to remember
- to stimulate deeper thought in an area
- to explore feelings

- to change the subject
- to defuse stress
- to check for understanding
- to explore core objections and reasons behind them
- to lead the prospect toward your unique, strong selling points

When combined with reflective listening, the best probing questions give the other person new insights. The skilled questioner will guide the discussion along the path she selects, while building arguments in favor of her proposal.

Closed Questions

The purpose of closed probes is to get specific information and to get short answers. Closed probes are answered by a word, a number or a range of numbers, a time, or *yes* or *no*.

For example: "Did you attend the meeting?" "What time is the meeting?"

Closed probes usually begin with words such as *When, Where, Who, How Many, Which, How Much, How Long, Are you*, or *Will you*. They request specific, brief information. If you ask a closed probe to a person who does not talk much, you are almost sure to get a very brief answer. If you ask a closed probe with an inviting tone to a person who tends to talk a lot, you may get a longer answer, as they may be encouraged to elaborate on the short answer.

Closed questions are useful for controlling the conversation, and they are efficient. However, they can shut down dialogue and make a discussion sound like an interrogation.

Open Questions

Open probes, on the other hand, invite longer answers. They are used to explore thoughts, feelings, and attitudes.

For example:

- What do you think about this?

- What are your feelings about that?
- What methods would you use?
- Would you give me an example of that?
- Can you give me a picture of this?
- Would you elaborate on that?
- Would you share with me your opinion on this?
- Could you tell me about that?

These questions tend to get longer, more revealing answers, especially if the answers are followed up with further open or closed questions. Examples of follow-up questions include:

- Can you tell me a bit more about that?
- How did that work?
- Are there any other reasons for that?

Sometimes, asking for just a bit more information will give you a lot more.

The advantage of open questions is clear. They allow the prospect to elaborate and explore the response as they wish. The disadvantage is that they take longer, and the questioner may lose some control.

Ideally, you ask almost all open questions. Then, occasionally, you take some control with a closed question. For example:

- What are your major concerns in ordering? (answer — likely lengthy)
- Then, lead time and integration are the two major concerns? (closed — to summarize and take control).

One question construct useful in this regard is the *What-Which-Why*. This is a great technique to find the decision-making criteria in a nonthreatening way, to rank the importance, and also to learn the position in more depth.

Example:

- In making this contract decision, what are the issues that most concern you? (closed question: probable short answer or list)

- Which is the most important? (closed question: single answer)
- Why is that? (open probe: elicit further thoughts and feelings)

Direct and Indirect Questions

How obvious and straightforward can you afford to be with your questioning? This depends upon the relationship and status in the account. A direct question is to-the-point. There is no doubt of intent. However, it can be seen as threatening. Here are examples of direct questions:

- Who will make the decision?
- Why did you choose that supplier for the last deal?
- Is price important to you?

This blunt of a question carries risk. It may put the prospect off and stymie conversation. It may even hurt the relationship. In some cultures, it would be a major *faux pas*. Usually, it's best to use an indirect question instead.

An indirect question is less threatening and slightly less abrupt. It is lower-risk, and more likely to elicit a reply. It isn't as obvious, and might get the other person to volunteer more. However, it may be too subtle, and they may miss the point. Here are examples:

- Who will be involved in the buying process?
- Do you have other suppliers?
- What things are important in the buying decision?

Note these questions are parallel to the direct ones above. For the first one, you give the prospect a chance to save face if he will not be involved or make the decision. You potentially get more information, and you don't risk the relationship.

For the second question, rather than "putting the heat on" the prospect or his supplier, you are asking about all suppliers. Then, he can lead you to the specific supplier with whom you may be competing.

The third keeps the focus off price. Don't assume price is the main criteria. It helps you explore other important areas wherein you may agree more readily.

Now, we have four combinations of questions. This gives you great flexibility to control the conversation and to protect the relationship.

	Open	Closed
Direct	Tell me about your role in the decision-making process. How important is price?	Do you make the decision? Is price the major factor?
Indirect	How are buying decisions made? What criteria are important when considering a purchase of this type?	Is there a standard set of evaluation criteria and processes for deciding? What is most important when deciding?

When formulating your questions, use the quadrants above to decide from where best to probe. You will be a much more effective questioner.

"There aren't any embarrassing questions — just embarrassing answers."
- Carl Rowan

Questioning Process

Now that you have good methods to formulate your questions, consider what to ask, and in what order. I look at questioning as a funnel, wherein you start at the top with broad, open probes, and proceed to more specifics.

Start with general information questions, to build rapport and to get to know the customer's business better. The beauty of a really good question is that it eliminates assumptions. The first question could be as simple as, "Tell me about your business." Other examples that focus on different areas related to the situation analysis in section 1 might include:

-   Tell me about the industry.

-   What trends are affecting the business?

- What are the biggest challenges in growing your business?

- How does your decision-making process work?

- What do your customers want from you?

- Who is your major competitor?

- How long have you been with the company?

These are very broad questions by design. They force you to start with your potential customer's main area of interest: himself!

Now, before you ask questions, it's best if you tell the customer you've done some preliminary research. You are not coming to the meeting cold. Very quickly, you will determine what is important to the customer. You will determine the process and some of the key factors in the decision.

Now, move on to specific questions to determine needs, wants, requirements and expectations. These usually will be the logical determinants of business value. Ask about timing and specifications. Examples include:

- What are you looking for in a supplier?

- Please define your specs.

- What do you need from our team?

These questions help to build rapport. They are nonthreatening and fact-based. Expectations are a powerful influence. Once your prospect describes the criteria above, ask a follow-up question to get him to prioritize them for you.

When he answers these questions, he is telling you specifically what he is going to base his decision on. How could you begin to make an intelligent sales presentation without knowing what his decision is going to be based upon?

Now move into the competitive area. Ask how the current supplier or internal system is meeting their needs, and how well.

Examples might include:

- Who is your current supplier?

- How are you currently meeting these needs (e.g., if internally-supplied)?

- How well does your current supplier meet your needs?

Note that you may need to probe deeper if the prospect defers or hesitates to answer. Your job is to raise awareness. Do not castigate or bad-mouth the current competition. Create rapport and proceed carefully. You are helping the potential client to better understand.

Now, you can ask a good one:

- If you could change anything about your current supplier/product, what would you change?

This question is a powerful question, and if you are patient, you will be rewarded with a good response. Remember, nothing is perfect! Many times, the first response will be: "I can't think of anything." Be patient. Suggest a couple of specific ideas. For example, "How would you improve technical support?" Ask the question again in a different way, and wait patiently for the answer.

What you're searching for is that dissatisfaction, no matter how small it may be. Once identified, you have a starting point on which to build your presentation. People are always looking to improve their current situation. This is an opportunity question which will help you avoid assumptions.

Summarize

After conducting a questioning process, step back and summarize with the buyer. When you summarize needs, you show that you were listening, you verify understanding, and you build commitment to the fact that these really are needs.

Questioning Tips

- Ask one question at a time.

- Use the pause; value silence.

- Ask open questions most of the time.

- Know why you are asking questions; probe with a purpose.

- Be willing to ask a follow-up question.

- Take notes.

- Summarize.

Handling Questions

Some pitches are as much as half question-and-answer sessions. They can be tough. I find even the best presenters fear being "caught out" during these sessions. The *Four P's* enter the equation yet again: preparation counts! Do your positioning during your preparation. You are the expert. You know the most likely questions on the topic. I always ask presenters to prepare a list of at least the top 10 most likely questions and answers, and practice giving them verbally. You should ensure you have a good grasp of them, and can answer positively and readily, with good, open body language.

Resist the urge to elaborate and introduce new material in your answer. The purpose of Q&A is to clarify; not to make a new presentation. By the same token, keep your answers short and to-the-point. Your best answer is clearly presented in one minute or less.

What if you ask, "Any questions?" and get the dreaded silent treatment? There are two solutions. If you have a strong coach, he can ask one or two. Also, be prepared with a few of your own. The questions in the previous section would be a great place to start.

Ten Tips for Handling Questions

1. Be prepared: expect the usual issues of management, delivery, cost, contingencies, and handling problems to be brought up first.

2. Be yourself. Don't try to be someone you are not.

3. Keep your cool. Remain in control.

4. Watch your attitude. Treat it as a game. Smile.

5. Answer the questions as best you can, but ensure that your

answers include the key statements (differentiators, strong points) which you need to make.

6. Answer the core question: *yes, no, maybe*, bullet points. Keep it short.

7. Unclear answers lead to misinterpretation.

8. Verbose, rambling answers lead to misinterpretation.

9. Summaries aid accuracy.

10. Always do your best to understand your audience.

A Special Pitch: The Investor or Analyst Day

Top management personnel at many companies regularly have to present a specific type of pitch — the Investor or Analyst Tour. Unfortunately, many executives don't really see this as a pitch. The typical business manager sees them as a report of status and plans. Therefore, they see the objective as an "update" and don't use them as well as they can. These presentations are like typical business presentations in many ways, but they also differ in very important areas as well.

In reality, these events are a corporate "show" meant to let the analysts know that the company is doing well, that the management is competent, and that they're working together. They allow the company to showcase its strengths. They are therefore really a pitch — but with serious undertones regarding the business and its prospects and strategies.

The principles outlined in this book all are relevant. People buy with their hearts and their heads. They need to see a confident, coordinated, and connected management team. Good audience understanding; relevant, engaging messages; and confident answers are the order of the day.

So clarify the objective, focus your messages, differentiate your uniqueness in the market, and add evidence to back up what you are saying. It is high-stakes, high-pressure work, with commensurate rewards when done well.

The Audience

The audience can consist of Investors or Analysts, or a mix of both. Investors usually represent funds which actually own shares in the company. Investors traditionally are focused on strategies and performance driving longer-term shareholder wealth. They are sometimes called "buy side." Analysts are securities analysts, generally looking into the equity with an eye towards advisory. They may represent securities firms for whom they write reports recommending stocks. They tend to be more short-term, numbers- and models-focused. Analysts may be called "sell side."

Note that companies are not able (legally) to provide "forward-looking statements" in these talks. Therefore, the presenters cannot include forecasted results — history only. Also, be wary of revealing too much competitive information. Much of this information will go immediately on the Web, and management will need to use care to paint a picture without getting too many specifics on the performance of certain proprietary business areas. Analysts will push hard for numbers to put into their models.

So these pitches are all about ensuring the audience the team is competent, functioning well, and has a good strategy. It's a balancing act for the presenters — sell the sizzle of the future when you cannot really show the steak.

Hence, some presenters are very nervous and approach the work with a great deal of concern and fear. Some will focus on the words — getting the script "perfect." They feel that this is the way to stay out of trouble (and minimize the chances of a career-limiting move!). But this leads to robotic deliveries. It's best to be yourself — a confident, practiced, professional self.

> I learned a very apt analogy from a client while working with a management team. He said,
>
> "I can't read from a script. The guidelines are a frame. I cannot go outside it. But, what I paint inside the frame is up to me."

Presentation by Committee

Note also that these presentations will go through many, many iterations before reaching final stage. I often refer to them as "presentation by committee" with all the concomitant challenges and dilution that infers. While you may have a great story, finely honed and practiced, and fully ready to go, someone with a higher corporate rank can easily choose to change it. And someone else in the pecking order may change it again. Also note that Investor Relations and often the legal department will have a view. You may be asked to modify the message several times. You will be questioned about your material in relation to that of your peers. Slides will come and go. You may be asked not to present at all one day before the event.

One way this presentation differs from the norm is that, in this case, there really is a law that what is presented must be handed out (and put on the website). So you cannot strictly apply the normal advice regarding special handouts, different documents, etc. For better or worse, in this case, PowerPoint is king — much more than in the typical business presentation. Now, this doesn't mean you allow them to be a cluttered mess. It simply means you acknowledge that this tool is a primary communication mechanism. You still work for clarity in messaging, audiovisuals, and in spoken communications.

These always are team presentations, with all the moving parts and increased difficulties to make them more "interesting," which give your team more scope to fall or to shine. Working with your colleagues, understanding and acknowledging the others' messages, and referring to them in your message will show coordination. Park your ego outside.

Investor Relations or another internal group will usually provide a couple of items.

- Audience analysis — usually a detailed bio and perhaps also some reports written by the analyst.
- Q&A by business or presentation. This usually consists of a detailed set of questions and politically correct answers for the presenters. It is a useful document, but may be only skimmed as it can arrive late.

Note that usually the senior person will handle and allocate the questions. This works well. As discussed before, role play the Q&A and apply the *Four P's*.

Putting it All Together

The process of Pitching to Win can be represented physically as a Presentation Pyramid, starting from the bottom up, as in the figure on the next page.

Every presentation has four primary components:

1. The Words: The flow, structure, story, and grabbers, all supported by relevant objectives and audience understanding.

2. The Delivery: The skills of connection with the physical: eyes, voice, and body.

3. The Graphics: Relevant PowerPoints with minimal bullet points, drawings on white boards, and props.

4. The Q&A: Questioning, listening, and handling audience questions.

Winning Pitch professionals master all four components. Words are the foundation of your presentation. However, words alone are cold and lifeless — they don't appeal to the heart. Add effective team delivery, relevant and engaging graphics, and effective handling of questions, and your story will stand out in the crowd.

Presentation Pyramid

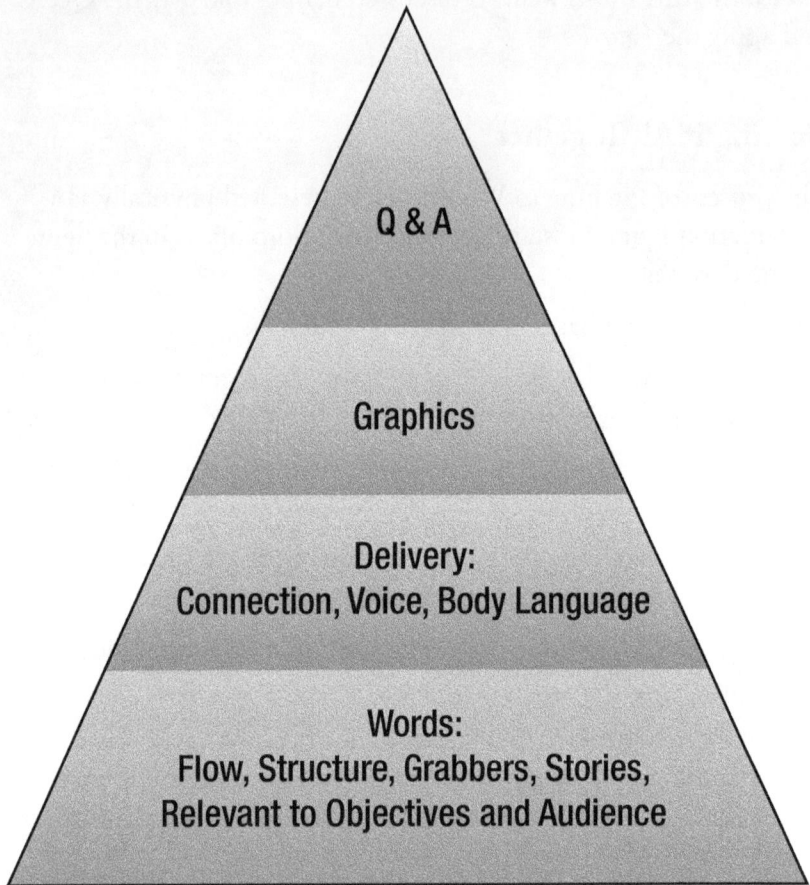

A solid foundation is important, and winning presentations build on all elements.

Summary

- Ensure a good first impression with preparation, concentration, and enthusiastic attention.

- Tame the jitters with physical and mental preparation.

- Look at people; not at screens or computers. Connect with the eyes.

- Modulate your voice tone to convey interest, enthusiasm, conviction and passion.

- Embrace the pause — to emphasize the wisdom of your message.

- Be careful about weak words.

- Gestures and movement are forms of universal language. They add emphasis, energy and excitement.

- Reflective listening is a powerful tool in the communication skill set.

- The quality of your life – and the success of your pitch — depends on the quality of your communication.

- Put it all together, building from the base of the Presentation Pyramid with a good story and adding engaging delivery skills, clear, relevant graphics, and effective Q&A.

Follow Through

"It ain't over 'til it's over."

- Yogi Berra

What can we do better?

"Sandwich every bit of criticism between two thick layers of praise."
- Mary Kay Ash

The easiest thing for a team to do after a pitch is to pack up and go their separate ways — "Glad that's over!" The Winning Pitch team doesn't take the easiest route; it takes the improvement route.

As soon as you get back to your office, spend focused time with the team asking the fundamental questions:

- Why did that work?
- Why didn't that go better?

Unless you do this honest debrief, your ability to improve will depend upon luck. This feedback requires time and effort. Ask for feedback from the team and anyone you can in the audience. Analyze both successes and failures. Be open to giving and receiving negative and positive feedback. Both have value.

Here is a checklist to help with the debriefing session:

- Did we do our background work well?
- Did we research and properly understand the prospect's team?
- Did our offer meet the needs (rational and emotional) expressed?
- Did we clearly show where our offer is ahead of the competition?
- Did we have the right people on our team?

- Did we have the right technical and functional support?

- Did we establish rapport? Did we demonstrate empathy?

- Was our pitch professionally presented? Did it grab and maintain interest?

- Did the presentation start well, flow clearly, and end strongly?

- Did the pitch meet our objectives?

- Did we demonstrate relevant benefits?

- Did we handle objections effectively?

- Did we respond well to questions?

- Did we leave them with relevant, key takeaway points?

- Did we ask for the business?

Feedback sessions can be challenging. The team probably has worked very long and hard, and often has a lot of ego invested. When giving feedback, be aware of the sensitivities and maintain everyone's self-confidence. You don't want to tear down the team, but to build up its strength.

Good feedback:

- Is solution-focused, not problem-focused.

- Involves the action, not the person.

- Focuses on the impact of the action, not only the action.

- Is descriptive, not judgmental.

- Is direct and clear.

Be understanding. Be clear and concise. This is not a place for speeches. Here are some examples which may assist you in giving better feedback.

Solution-focused

Your monotone is boring.

- To improve the audience's engagement, work to modulate your pace and tone.

Action-focused

You come across as a bully.

- By jumping in to answer, you sidelined us and undermined the sense of team unity. In the future, please let the moderator divide up the questions.

Impact-focused

You are not making eye contact.

- When you looked at the slides, you disengaged from the audience, and they were losing interest.

Descriptive

You looked like you didn't want to be there.

- I noticed that you seemed to almost disappear behind the podium, and your body language seemed apologetic. How do you think that came across?

Until the Fat Lady Sings

Until the contract is signed, sealed, and delivered, you still have a chance to win. Keep pitching.

Your ultimate objective is to get the business. The team's mindset should be that this presentation is another milestone on the road to the win — it may not be the finale. Many times, I have seen teams called back for more discussion.

You can often win a pitch because of something you do a few hours or a few days after the presentation. During your debrief, discuss any and all ways you can keep engaging with the prospect.

One person on your pitch team is tasked with taking note of anything that could provide a reason to keep on pitching afterwards. Keep track of all questions, objections, or suggestions made. Do any of them provide a new opportunity for interaction?

Maybe you can change some artwork to incorporate suggestions the client made during the presentation; make follow-up calls to the prospect to see what else he or she might want; research a concept that was brought up by the prospect during your pitch (perhaps by one of your competitors?) to prove if it's workable. Maybe you can review the fees. Keep pitching, because you haven't yet heard the first bars of the fat lady's song.

Summary

- Debrief: What went well? What can be improved?
- Keep engaging with the prospect. You never know when a new opportunity might present itself. "The opera ain't over till the fat lady sings".

Summary

"The common denominator of success — the secret of success of every person who has ever been successful — lies in the fact that 'They formed the habits of doing things that failures don't like to do.'"

- Albert E.N. Gray

"Success is the progressive realization of a worthy ideal."

- Earl Nightingale

Success in any endeavor is not about great breakthroughs, brilliance, hard work or talent. Nothing is more common than smart, talented people who are unsuccessful. Most successful people are of average intelligence and skill, but they possessed more important characteristics. Dr. Charles Garfield reported on 20 years of research in his book, *Peak Performers*. According to Garfield, peak performers in all walks of life:

- Are not born — they are made.

- Are average people.

- Are committed to results, not activities.

Successful people do small things to achieve their goals every day. High achievers in all areas attribute their success to passion, vision, and mission —not to *aptitude*, but to *attitude* — not to *education*, but to *application*.

No professional athlete would consider rising to the top without years of work and coaching. If you want to move to the top, make a commitment to learning from the best. Actively seek out professional guidance by reading, taking classes, and employing a professional coach.

There is an immense need in the world today for great communicators. There is a critical shortage of *real* communication — communication that touches the heart and the head. We need communicators who share human values and goals. We need presenters who encourage and advocate compelling action. People who can command and compel an audience are sought after the world over.

Very few people are willing to invest the time and effort to excel. Will you?

I sincerely hope you now have an appreciation of the impact good presentations can have on your business and personal life. Good communicators touch and change lives. They redirect companies. They command countries. You can be one of them.

The techniques and practices for achieving excellent outcomes are in your hands. Make them your own with application and practice. Get professional guidance. In all walks of life, you will greatly advance yourself *Pitching to Win*.

In a land far, far away lived three boys who were always up to no good — constantly getting in trouble, always playing tricks on friends and family members.

In that land was a Wise Old Man, a hermit that lived at the top of a mountain. People said he was the wisest person in all the land.

Well, on this day the boys were bored — very bored. They were just looking for trouble. Or was trouble looking for them?

They decided to play a trick on the Old Man, but couldn't think of anything. So they thought, and thought, and thought…

And finally one of the boys had an idea. "What if we were to catch a bird? We can take the bird up the mountain to the wise old man, put the bird behind our back and ask him a question. We could say, 'Mr. Wise Old Man, I have a bird behind my back, and I have a simple question for you. Is the bird dead or alive?'

"If the Wise Old Man says, 'it's dead,' we can bring our hands from behind our back and let the bird go - proving the wise old man is wrong.

"If he says, 'it's alive,' we can snap the bird's neck and say 'Sorry, the bird is dead,' again proving him wrong."

So the boys wandered through the fields until they caught a bird. Then, they climbed up the mountain until they found the old man.

One of the boys asked, "Mr. Wise Old Man, we have a question for you. Behind my back is a bird. Is the bird dead or alive?"

You know what the Wise Old Man said?

"Boys — the future of that bird is in your hands."

The moral of this story is that your future is in your hands. You have a choice. You alone can use the talent you have. Will you?

NOTES

1. Richard Restak, *The New Brain: How the Modern Age is Rewiring Your Mind* (Rodale, 2004).

2. R. Miller and S. Heiman, Strategic Selling (New York: Warner Books Inc., 1986).

3. Garr Reynolds, *Presentation Zen* (Berkley: New Riders, 2008), 45.

4. http://en.wikipedia.org/wiki/Minimalism

5. John Medina, *Brain Rules* (Seattle, Washington: Pear Press, 2008).

6. Wills, Garry, *Lincoln at Gettysburg: The Words That Remade America* (New York: Simon & Schuster, 1992).

7. http://en.wikipedia.org/wiki/Spacing_effect

Testimonials for Jeff Woodard

Jeff has a low key effective coaching style that benefits both mid level and senior executives who would like to work on improving their communication , pitching and presentation skills. He has worked with some senior team leaders and is an excellent player - coach to senior managers . I have attended his multi-day training session on presentation skills and also worked with him on creating individual speeches for small and large audiences. If you want to be expertly prepared and deliver a consciously crafted speech that achieves your predetermined goals, then you need Jeff.

Vivek Goyal,
Managing Director,
Head of Business & Relationship Management Group, Asia Pacific

"If you think speaking to an audience does not require goal setting, preparation, rehearsals and feedback you do not need to work with Jeff. If you, however, want to be expertly prepared and deliver a consciously crafted speech that achieves your predetermined goals, then you need Jeff. I have attended his multi-day training session and also worked with him on creating individual speeches for small and large audiences. He is a fantastic coach who helped me become a better and relaxed speaker but also improved the impact of any single speech we worked on together by 200%. Highly recommended!"

Chris Werner,
Global Head Strategy, Business Development (M&A) &
Bancassurance at Standard Chartered Bank

"Public speaking, like writing, is always improved by a good editor. No matter how experienced one is, Jeff can help you become a more effective public speaker. He has a very gentle, low-key coaching style that is highly effective, perhaps because he doesn't push but rather nudges -- "you might want to think about this," "let's see how this changes the effect..." He's worked with some very senior executives, and many of them are now amongst the region's most highly regarded public orators. If you're looking for a good presentation coach for senior managers, give Jeff a call."

Patricia Bjaaland Welch,
Director of External Relations at McKinsey & Co., Inc

"The quality of our communications directly affects the quality of our lives." How about you? Are you maximizing your persuasive communication opportunities?

To get clear on your personal and team goals and what it will take to get the winning edge, contact me about setting up a free 30-minute session where you will walk away with specific steps about what you can do to achieve your goals.

Contact Jeff at **jeff@jnwoodard.com** or call +65 9786-3062

www.jwoodard.net
www.jeff-woodard.com
www.woodard.asia
www.thewinningpitch.info
www.thewinningpitch.biz

About the Author

Jeff Woodard is a leading expert on effective presentation skills, leadership image development, and communications and media skills. He is a founder and Partner in Simitri Pte Ltd, in Singapore, a communications consultancy with offices across Asia. Simitri develops and delivers unique products and services to enable clients to accelerate success, both personally and professionally. Jeff's private clients include executives at many of the top companies in the world, including Dell Computer, Microsoft, Standard Chartered Bank, JP Morgan, Deutsche Bank, and BHP Billiton. He has mentored and coached business leaders in dozens of countries. Jeff's knowledge and expertise make him a sought-after corporate communications speaker and coach.

Jeff has coached executives to clarify their messages, and to present them with impact for IPO road shows, stock analyst and investor presentations, board meetings, large annual business meetings and trade shows, as well as for internal and external events. His techniques have helped thousands of people develop and deliver their mission-critical business presentations.

An expert on formulating message content and teaching clear and passionate delivery, Jeff's focus includes executive training and coaching to quickly improve his clients' awareness, understanding, and impact in all areas of their lives. Jeff co-developed The Winning Pitch Workshop, which consists of two days of training followed by 1:1 pitch coaching. He and his partners have delivered it successfully to hundreds of business people over the past four years, in the US, Europe, Asia, and the Middle East.

With a strong international business background, Jeff focuses on bottom-line results. He holds a degree in Electrical Engineering, and an MBA. He is a charter member of the Asia Professional Speaker's Association of Singapore, and a member of the International Coach Federation.

Jeff believes in giving more value than expected, and is dedicated to his motto, "The quality of our communications directly affects the quality of our lives." We are communicating most of our waking hours; we can always learn to do it better.

A father of two sons and one daughter, Jeff has lived and worked internationally for 20 years; he currently lives with his family in Singapore.

To get clear on your personal and team goals and what it will take to get the winning edge, contact me about setting up a free 30-minute session where you will walk away with specific steps about what you can do to achieve your goals.

For more information or to set up your complimentary session, email Jeff at **jeff@jnwoodard.com,** visit the web site, or call +65 9786-3062

www.ingramcontent.com/pod-product-compliance
Lightning Source LLC
Chambersburg PA
CBHW030015290326
41934CB00005B/353